AF560857

The Fictional World of
Saul Bellow

The Fictional World of Saul Bellow

Ishteyaque Shams

Published by
ATLANTIC
PUBLISHERS & DISTRIBUTORS (P) LTD
7/22, Ansari Road, Darya Ganj,
New Delhi-110002
Phones : +91-11-40775252, 23273880, 23275880, 23280451
Fax : +91-11-23285873
Web : www.atlanticbooks.com
E-mail : orders@atlanticbooks.com

Branch Office
5, Nallathambi Street, Wallajah Road,
Chennai-600002
Phones : +91-44-64611085, 32413319
E-mail : chennai@atlanticbooks.com

ISBN 978-81-269-1687-0

Printed in India at Glorious Printers, A-13, D.S.I.D.C., Jhilmil Industrial Area, Delhi-110095

Preface

When I started teaching Saul Bellow's *Dangling Man* to my students, I went through other novels of Bellow too and seriously realized that there was a dearth of books on Saul Bellow's novels which might be helpful to and useful for the teachers as well as students. Considering this point of view I decided to write such a book which might elaborate and critically explain all Bellow's novels and short stories just in one volume. For this I read all his novels and short stories and felt that though realism and naturalism are, no doubt, main factors in the making of his fictional imagination, yet romanticism too has a great influence over it. His insistence upon the uniqueness and importance of the individual, his stress upon the intuitional nature of knowledge, his realization of the insufficiency of science to explain the mystery of life, his call for a rebellion against the tyranny of social savagery, his belief in the infinite potentiality of human existence and his sense of obligation of every individual to live up to the very best in him, indicate his attitude and inclination towards romanticism. He drew nourishment and vigour from the great Russian writers, from Indian philosophy and religious thought as well as from Jewish and American culture.

Bellow has been a very popular writer and his books have attracted readers in large number. His popularity is not conditioned so much by his descriptions of American social disturbances or chaos in his books as by something that lies hidden behind the descriptions. Truly enough, Bellow is a writer of an era of chaos and disillusionment, but his approach is neither defeatist nor negative in nature; instead, it is something vigorously optimistic and positive in spirit.

The book will be useful for the students and teachers of English literature in general and English fiction in particular. Besides, it will immensely help the researchers of Saul Bellow. To those who wish to deeply understood Saul Bellow and his fictional world, it will provide for a richly rewarding reading.

I would like to thank my colleagues for their sincere co-operation and my wife, Mumtaz Parveen and my children, Aiman and Sana for relieving me from domestic affairs during this period. I am also thankful to M/s Atlantic Publishers and Distributors, New Delhi, particularly Dr. K.R. Gupta, Honorary Advisor, for the interest evinced in bringing out this book.

Ishteyaque Shams

Contents

1
Introduction

Saul Bellow, the winner of three National Book Awards for fiction and the recipient of Nobel Prize for literature, has a unique background. He is a Jew, a second generation Russian, a graduate in Anthropology, a teacher, a twice divorced husband, "a dreamier sort of a creature",[1] an outsider looking at United States, yet finally a true American. Born in 1915 he witnessed two world wars and weathered the depression and ultimately committed suicide in 2005. He has been voicing honestly and artistically, the poverty of the soul in the land of plenty, leaving his impact on the book of life as well as literature. Nevertheless, he is a typical product of his time and is hailed as a writer of immense achievement. More than ten novels of assured success, twenty odd short stories, a fairly large number of essays and lectures, and a few plays constitute a healthy body of literature which no serious student of English literature in general and American literature of twentieth century in particular can ignore.

The time he belonged to is the time when the Jews and even Roman Catholics were trying to establish themselves in White Anglo-Saxon Protestant America. America was on the road to prosperity. Scientific advances, huge production and a dominating position in the world politics made America proud, confident and self-sufficient. Yet the same turned to disadvantage also. "Scientific management turned factory workers into dehumanized automatons."[2] They required even fewer skills, and were involved in endless, repetitive jobs, which made them feel out of place, unwanted and alienated.

This led to unemployment also, which is another cause of their growing feelings of dissatisfaction and insecurity in life.

Influenced by the values of work ethics one's status in that American Society was determined by the fact, whether one was working or not, the nature of the job, and the compensation for it. As a general rule, higher paid individuals were thought to have greater personal worth than those receiving less pay and doing menial jobs. Consequently, a person, without pay became worthless, was ignored and undermined by others and rebuked and victimized by himself. This degradation of the sell became a serious problem and threatened the very existence of the society. It required immediate redeeming. There was a basic conflict between the self that demanded preservation and society that demanded sacrifice of the self.

The period following First World War was the age of anxiety, disillusionment, chaos, disbelief and utter despair. Life became surprisingly vast, unbelievably scattered and left loose from the moulds and traditions. Old faiths were almost dead, new sustaining forces were yet to be discovered.

The American public did not enter the war in 1941 with the same naïve idealism, they had shown in 1917, and as a result, they were less affected by a post war disillusionment. Still there had been an incessant complaint of a nagging sense of anxious insecurity for a long time. In the twenty years between the world wars they "passed through contrasting emotional stages at home, from an over confident positiveness to a chastened negativity".[3]

In matters of religion, "secularization of beliefs and attitudes spread as rapidly among the Jews as among the Protestants".[4] Catholics remained more devout, for them the church became a symbol of continuity in an alien environment, though it lasted only for a short while. Instead of some abrupt shock, religious faith continued to ebb slowly. People would not object now to the inter-faith marriages of their offspring. "Now one Jew out of three marries a gentile."[5] People continued to go to the church, but it was more or less a social meeting ground. In this area, individualism seemingly functioned as a value. It was not supposed good manners to question anyone's beliefs.

In general, there was a loss of certitudes in the high matters of religion and ethics, and a widespread disagreement about the first principles in life as well as in literature. Chaos and disorder of individual life were reflected in literature too. While in life it was a problem of "how to live and what to live for"?,[6] in literature it was a problem of what to write about, and for whom to write?

Gradually, however, there was a turn away from sceptical materialism, and inclination towards a search for spiritual satisfaction.

> In case of general public, it took the form of a well-publicized and widely acclaimed return to religion—an increase in church going, a heightened in theology and much talk about putting god back in education.[7]

Although one can never be sure, whether it was a revival of genuine religious feelings or nearly a neurotic escapism caused by the general insecurity of the age.

The American involvement in Vietnam and Southern Asia had eaten away at the moral fibre of the American people for more than a decade. Their foreign policy devoid of any morality exposed themselves to themselves. But the greatest shock came with the triple assassinations of President Kennedy in November 1963, Martin Luther King in April 1968 and Senator Robert Kennedy in June 1968. Their consciousness received its most shattering blows. Crimes like murders, kidnappings, perverted sex attitudes of the younger generation and the disintegration of the family unit started blowing American society into pieces. It was as if not having to do much for their basic needs, they employed themselves into these adventurous, thrilling, anti-social activities. There was no social harmony so to say.

Thus, man was left to find the meaning of life within himself unaided by others. Even in this world of automation and computerized thought, an intellectual declined to acknowledge defeat. They carried on their search for the recovery of the moral certainty and rediscovery of its traditional ideals of individuality. They could pulse the deep restlessness of the American public Leslie Fiedler to believe that

> In the post-war period of the atomization, uprooting, and universal alienation, the image of the Jews tends to become the image of everyone.[8]

Literature of this period reflected this upheaval and fermentation. Realism and Naturalism had become dominant modes by 1930. Pessimism was the natural consequence and the most obvious sign of the widespread decay of faith. Whereas the spirit of the ancient tragedy was ultimately that of reverant acceptance, the spirit of the modern is like Conrad's of ironic aloofness, like Hardy's of vehement protest, like Hemingway's of alcoholic bravado, like Dreiser's of complete confusion and utter dismay. The dangers of such pessimism were obvious enough, it may simply depress human vitality and dry up the springs of energy at their very source. This danger was looming large with the literature of the earlier half twentieth century.

Yet to call this a demoralized, devalued, or a pessimistic age is to miss the most significant activity of the age. As the decade of fifties progressed, it began to become apparent that a sort of catharsis was being achieved and there was a sincere effort on the part of Bernard Malamud, John Updike, Edward Albee, Saul Bellow and others to synthesize and to simplify. The twentieth century writers started struggling to make some sense out of a seeming senseless world, if not senseless at least a world sloughing off old values and labouring for the new ones. This grouping in the dark explains the grotesqueries of Carson Macullers, the violence of Norman Mailer, the anguish of Bernard Malamud, the ironies of John Barth, the bitterness of James Baldwin and the questing, searching spirit of Saul Bellow. In the latter half of the twentieth century, they are all searching in their own way, for some new definitions of what it means to be human and thus Bellow is well within the main stream of modern American literature. Saul Bellow's third novel, *The Adventures of Augie March* (1953) is a curious parable of the course of American literary realism. This novel opens in the Chicago slums and ends with the exotics and expatriates of Mexico and Europe. The most touchingly emphatic episode in the latter half of the novel is that of the cowardly, eagle Caligula who simply refuses to play out his Darwinian and Hemingwayish role as an eagle.

Bellow realized from the very first that if literature is to be a current and constant force, it should intimately be connected with life—life of a common man. And at the same time, it should provide him with food for higher self, his spiritual being, if it intends to remain in the very centre of life and not driven to the periphery. He recognized the immense desire of the general public for what was simple and true. He knew this also that literature, to a great degree, will have to replace religion.

Bellow believed that

> Almost nothing of a spiritual ennobling character is brought into the internal life of a modern American by his social institutions. Society feeds him, clothes him, to an extent protects him, and he is its infant. If he accepts the state of infancy, contentment can be his, but if the idea of higher functions comes to him, he is profoundly unsettle.[9]

The universe seems secure only to those who do not question too far. Dissatisfaction, uneasiness, want, is the sign of the existence of a superior being along with our animal nature. The novels of Bellow provide us with honest questioning, searching and probing in the heart of the darkness, each novel taking us into a different uncharted territory.

Each novel of Bellow creates its own category. He is too great a genius to adhere to, and be bound by one particular tradition, yet it is obvious that the structure of his fiction is built upon the works of his predecessors as well as his contemporaries. His own development as an individual man and as an author will also have to be taken into account. He is:

> One of those figures of the 1930s who have not repudiated their heritage and their link with central literary tradition of the past.[10]

There have been efforts by different critics to relate Bellow with different movements in the world of fiction. Many of them are out to prove that he is actually under the influence of Kafka, Dostoevsky, Camus, Sartre, Nietzsche, Walt Whitman, James Joyace and Mark Twain. Helen Weinberg who finds a lot common between Franz Kafka and Bellow says, "Bellow seems most clearly concerned with Kafkan questions".[11] Jonathan Baumback places all the three novels of Bellow: *Dangling Man* (1944), *The Victim* (1947) and *Seize the Day* (1956)—which he calls "The novels of depth and claustrophobic internal exploration—under the influence of Dostoevsky".[12] Robert Gorham Davis says, "*Dangling Man*...is in the form of a diary, a rather Kafkaesque diary".[13] Irving Malin finds that "*Dangling Man* echoed of Dostoevsky and Kafka".[14] He has further linked Bellow's first two novels with Camus' *The Stranger* and Sartre's *Nausea*. Ihab Hassan says: "The characters in *The Victim* remain somewhat in the shadow realism between the ideal figures of Kafka and the 'real' characters of Dostoevsky".[15] There is no doubt that his novels "were shaped of course by the forces all lined up and waiting for all the novelists",[16] as has been pointed out by Marcus Klein. Ihab Hassan and Harper Howard are of the opinion that the "pattern of experience in Bellow is largely existential".[17] Peter M. Axthelm connects Bellow with "confessional novel".[18]

After reading Bellow's fiction and taking into account all these critical statements I find myself in a perfect position as well as agreement with Helen Weinberg who says that

> Bellow discredits the adoption, by the novelist, of a particular ideology or external structure of ideas about the world, even such an open philosophical system as Sartre's existentialism or Camu's idea of the absurd.[19]

I, on my part, would like to add that if he has the energy, exuberance and wonder of Whitman and Mark Twain; Nietzsche and Dostoevsky, are equally familiar with his imagination. If Bellow has taken up Whitman's joy in the free human spirit, he also has absorbed Dreiser's far-reaching and vastly honest urban determinism.

Realism and Naturalism are, no doubt, main factors in the making of his fictional imagination, yet romanticism too has a great influence over it. His insistence upon the uniqueness and importance of the individual, his stress upon the intuitional nature of knowledge, his realization of the insufficiency of science to explain the mystery of life, his call for a rebellion against the tyranny of social savagery, his belief in the infinite potentiality of human existence and his sense of obligation of every individual to live up to the very best in him, indicate his attitude and inclination towards romanticism. Whitman—pessimistic as to American fact, optimistic as to American possibilities—discusses a crucial paradox in his *Domestic Vistas*. This very paradox is very much at the heart of Bellow's work. He drew nourishment and vigour from the great Russian writers and, I doubt not, from Indian philosophy and religious thought as well as from Jewish and American culture.

Jewish cultural background contributed to Bellow's belief in men and an alliance to life. It has served as an armour against the despair resulting from the blows inflicted on the Jewish community throughout history. In my opinion, his popularity with American and continental public is mainly based upon this feeling. The sense of the holiness of everyman, of course not limited to the Jewish tradition alone but was sustained longer in the insulated semi-medieval Jewish community than among the Christians. At a time when basic values and old-world traditions of westerners lost their power, and community became fluid, his novels present a world in which sorrow is meaningful. They present a personal with-a-core, in a society where man had become all layers and without a centre. Ralph Ellison made a profound statement to a group of college English teachers assembled in 1970. He said that all American literature is the literature of minorities. Tony Tanner says the same thing when he says that in America today "the most important and central fiction is being written by Jewish writers".[20]

In the ordinary sense of the word 'Jewish authors', which we use for Malamud or Philip Roth we cannot use for Bellow, while the heroes in their novels fulfil their destiny by embracing Jewish traditions, the heroes of Bellow seem intent on escaping the bounds of that tradition. Bellow is not concerned with the problem like what it is to be a Jew but he is meditating upon more universal question like what it is to be a man, a human being. The essential point is that for Bellow Jewish tradition is meant to define and not to determine.

Bellow has been charged for not representing the Jew in the right perspective. Theodore J Rose says:

> Bellow by equating the Jew and the gentile in *The Victim* refuses to acknowledge basic inequalities and thus remains false to his heritage.[21]

But the same indifference—as we call it—has earned his name too. His objective outlook has been praised warmly by many. Henry Fairlie, on reading Bellow's *To Jerusalem and Back* (1976) gives his impression thus:

> Not for a moment does your Jewishness drops away from you, but neither does your Americanness; and in this there lies, I think, the expected but still achieved integrity of your book.[22]

Bellow resents enacting a role thrust upon him of being a Jew, which for him is 'an ideal construction'—if not of the Lord, then of the Community—he finds difficult to grow within this limit. He himself has mentioned this in *Jerusalem Post Weekly*:

> I will say one further thing about the Jewish writers in America, and that is that the Jewish Community in America was delighted when the Jewish Writers appeared on the scene because they felt that it would be good for the Jews in America. This puts us in a rather awkward position of doing public relations, unwillingly, for the American Jews.... And this was extremely disagreeable because it seemed to me to be an imposition on truth to have to make things come out nicely.[23]

But the nature of such a demand could not make Bellow react and retaliate which shows, how mature he is, how cool and balanced he can be. Neither he accepted the challenge, nor felt provoked and goes on directed by his own attitude and judgement. He further says:

> I always refuse to be provoked or challenged and simply went my stubborn, mulish, narrow way, without accepting either the task of making good public relations for the Jews or reacting strongly against the demand.[24]

Although he finds nothing foreign in the hats, sidelocks and fringes of the Hasids and he states that to see them is to have his 'Childhood revised', yet he can equally strongly put forward the opposite view-point. Still close family ties, especially the father-son relationship, the less important place of woman in the family, the over-riding sense of the ridiculous which manifests themselves in his novels have certainly their origin in Jewish cultural tradition.

Maxwell Geismar thinks that Judaism in Bellow's work is not only a source of nostalgia but also of guilt and anxiety rather than of pride and pleasure. According to him, "it is a constrictive and disturbing force rather than an enlarging and emancipating force".[25] What I find is that the sense of community is very strong in Jewish culture which may check the sense of alienation in an individual. Bellow himself seems to have a good amount of such sense and there is a good amount of resistance towards the claim of twentieth century apocalyptic romanticism, and there is a strong probability that this might be due to his Jewish background.

However, the American influence on him is equally powerful and "with Bellow an American of any experience could feel that he was in the midst of the life he knew".[26] Having received an orthodox religious education Bellow nevertheless experienced a relaxation of traditional lies as they dissolved in the secularism of his American surrounding. He has been nurtured on the democratic and individual tradition of America, he is proud of being an American. He writes in *To Jerusalem and Back*:

> I had not liked it when David Ben Gurion, on his visits to the United States, would call upon the American Jews to give up their illusions about goyish democracy and immigrate full speed to Israel. As if America's two hundred year record of liberal democracy signified nothing.[27]

This, shows how deeply he has imbibed American spirit. Apart from this, his choice of comedy rather than complaint seems to be affected by this American influence, because America being a land of new hope, tragedy seems to be out of place there.

Thus it should be obvious that although he assimilated in his being his Russian heritage, his Jewish upbringing and his American surrounding, yet he cannot exclusively be called to have belonged to one particular tradition or movement. His own knowledge, his own experience is the greatest source of his imagination and the profoundest influence on him is of his own understanding, intuition and original thinking. Alfred Kazim sounds this thing when he says that Bellow's novels are not the familiar material of American Naturalism neither does it resemble even the European tradition of the novel, Bellow would like to follow but "it is distinctly a world of his own".[28]

Saul Bellow pretends to be only a popular entertainer but even to a casual reader it soon becomes obvious that he is a writer with a purpose. He says, "it is not the didactic purpose itself which is a bad thing, and the modern novelist drawing back from the dangers of didacticism had often been strangely unreal".[29] For him, his vision of life is important, his interpretation, his choice and rendering of the events, and not the way or manner he does it, consequently, he picks up themes of contemporary interests and deals with them in his own extraordinary original way, delineating each of them with his own impressions of man and his destiny.

Saul Bellow's first novel *Dangling Man* (1944) is written on the age-old theme of war, but in treatment it is—to borrow the phrase from Leslie Fidler—'fresh beyond all expectations'. It is unlike any American war—book before or after, it was acclaimed by the critics of *Partisan Kenyon Review Orbit* as "an unassailable moral effort".[30] Bellow has realized that for his generation war itself was an anti-climax, that their real experience was the waiting, the dangling, the indecision, common-men, and whose surname we never come to know, has resigned from his job at the Inter-American Travel Bureau, to answer the army's call for induction. For the time being he has nothing to do, no regular job to attend to, no social role to play and no position to be proud of. He is now supported by his wife Iva, and gradually develops a sort of complex misinterpreting her demands which she has every right to make on a husband. His own brother and sister-in-law are also to him like strangers. In the name of self-respect he declines their offers of every kind. He cannot behave normally with any of his acquaintances. He, is free from any responsibility, has all the time and liberty to pursue his intellectual interests of reading and writing but this liberty he is unable to manage. He is aware all the time, that he is deteriorating and getting more and more dispirited, "storing bitterness and spite which eat like acids",[31] at the endowment of generosity and goodwill. He is deserted by everybody or vice versa but the result is that he is all alone in his agony, misery and moral confusion when it becomes undurable he asks the draft board to enlist him immediately. In this way, he ends his dangling by surrendering his freedom.

His second novel *The Victim* (1947) is on the anti-semite theme the perpetual victimization of the Jew by the gentiles. But this again has been handled by Bellow in an unanticipated and unexpected way. Leventhal, the hero, is much the victim of gentiles as well as of his own sense of right and wrong. Allbee, the anti-semite, accuses the Jew, Leventhal, of getting on in the world at his expense, solidifying his position by ruining Allbee's chance in life. Allbee introduces Leventhal who is jobless and in search of some work, to his boss Mr. Rudiger. The interview ends in a row but Leventhal forgets all about it after getting a suitable job at other place. Allbee thinks that he was fired by his boss on account of this and lost his job. His wife too leaves him and is killed in some accident. Allbee is a drunkard also and this may be a reason for his dismissal by his boss and his separation from his wife. Years after Allbee comes and claims Leventhal's attention help and compassionate treatment. Leventhal sees that though the particular accusation is groundless, because he never believed in it, yet there can be some truth in the general assumption that everyone progresses in this world at the expense of others. He never confesses it but guilt-ridden, he helps Allbee grudgingly, has a soft corner for him, yet fears him. He is caught unaware, his wife, who could soothe and console him, advise and guide him, is on vacation with her mother. His nephew falls sick and he is required to attend on him in the absence of his brother. The boy is shifted to the hospital, against the wishes of his mother and grandmother, dies there, and Leventhal partly accuses himself for his death. At the same time, he has a persistent feeling of insecurity. He comes to realize that it is only a chance that he belonged to the class of people 'who got away with it' who were lucky and successful. He might very well have belonged to the other class and may do so anytime in future because there is no justice anywhere. It is all a chance. Thus Leventhal is the eternal jew, accepting his moral responsibility for a world he never made. Overcome by treachery and malice in the social air around him, he struggles desperately, not indeed to go ahead, to make progress, but simply to exist, to survive.

The most original and interesting part of the novel is the description of Leventhal not only as a victim but as a victimizer as well. Bellow alone among our novelists has the sheer nerve to portray the Jew as a victimizer as well as a victim. Thus Allbee becomes a desirable focus on Leventhal's ordinary human guilt. Ultimately he is able to decide the extent of his responsibility towards himself and towards other human beings. His wife comes back as soon as his ordeal ends. In the end he is having a better paid job, a better looking personality and his wife, Mary is pregnant. Thus there is every possibility for a happy life yet he is still in doubt, uncertain, and still wonders 'who runs things, who, is at the back of all this big show?'

Bellow's third novel *The Adventures of Augie March* (1953) can be taken as a picaresque novel in the native tradition of Mark Twain, but it is directed and controlled by deeper concerns with the publication of this novel. There came not only a change in Bellow's writing but in the course of American novel itself. Here the world is no longer a mere proof of his hero's ability to see, to hear and to feel but it independently flames out in colours and sounds with all its joy and possible glory. History and richness of tradition are this novel's new hangings. Bellow "has rediscovered Fielding and Balzac and Dickens and Twain and *Moby Dick's Melville*".[32] Augie March, an aged man looks back towards the past and narrates the different adventures of his life. Augie has never seen his father, his family lives on charity and is supported by the worldly advice and guidance of grand ma, Laush who is really not connected with the family in any way. Different odd jobs are offered to him, right from bathing and feeding a luxury dog to entertaining a virgin of a rich family. His brother wants to train him for his coal business, Rentings want to adopt him, and almost everybody wants to thrust his ideas upon Augie. But Augie is obstinate in his own way. After a short trial, he leaves every offer. He is really in search of a 'fate good enough', and this search is endured peculiarly difficult by the nature of the world he is born into and has to move through. He really never finds any-thing to warrant a positive commitment. Throughout the novel he preserves to be himself by saying 'no' to the people and thus he is independent of the world like a picaro. Augie ventures into the world but he is not a part of it. His constant movement, shifting his positions, changing his jobs is an evasion than any engagement with this world. But to be home in a destructive unaccommodative world, the picaro must be hard boiled and resistant. Augie is resistant but not hard boiled. He is good-hearted, spontaneous and vulnerable. All along he is restless, unhappy and lonely. Unable to reach his ideal in life, married to an unfaithful ambitious wife and tied to a corrupt business he is far from achieving a fate good enough. But the important thing is that in the face of these circumstances he refuses to be disappointed. His answer to the rigours of destiny is a sarcastic laugh.

Bellow's next novel *Seize the Day* (1956) is on the failed salesman theme which celebrates unworthy Tommy Wilhelm. He left his studies and went to Hollywood to become a star against the advice of everybody and against his own better judgement. He, proved there to be a failure, joins a company manufacturing toy pens, leaves his job when suppressed by mother person. At present, he is jobless, separated from his wife and children, scolded, unhelped by his father, he is in a hopeless condition. He is brought to believe that money is everything in this world and without it finds himself worthless, an utter failure and consequently useless. There is a vivid realization of the New York City which has become strangely unfamiliar to its inhabitants, they are not used to New York any more, not even the natives. Every little thing is a strain there, where 'but to think is to be full of sorrow'. Life there is now devoid of any personal touch, it is only stress and strain. New York's unbearably hot weather, its crimes and murders, scarcity of parking place, worry over getting a ticket, its keen competition, its unimaginable crowd all are enough to cause ones' heart failure. And this whole New York City scene is, of course, an ironic parody of American society as a whole. Tommy, the fragmented individual, who has lost his job with Rojex Company, whose father has abandoned him, whose wife is bent upon teaching a lesson, whose children are strangers to him, who is living now on unicap and coca-cola, is one of the natural misfits, one of the loose objects on the social scene. Yearning for love he is one of the representative figures of a modern man.

Wilhelm is doubtless a failure, yet this kind of failure, he holds, is not the final reality. He believes that the soul's business must be different from the world's business. What is important in the novel is that confused and perplexed as he is, he has discovered his need to know his real self, which is the beginning of salvation.

His next novel *Henderson the Rain King* (1959) looks like a romantic, adventure story but that is the Bellownian way again—the use of popular form to make surprising statements about human soul. It is Bellow's Karamazove novel. He tries to move his hero into situations which like Dostoevsky's allow for endlessly intricate dialogue. Like today, Henderson is big, restless, wealthy, confused, given to exaggerated utterances, afraid of death, and most significantly obsessed with the need for salvation.

Henderson, a rich Jew, is a graduate of an Ivy League University, yet he is the author of a pig kingdom. At birth he weighed fourteen pounds and grown up, he was six feet four inches tall, two hundred and thirty pounds weight, he has an enormous head, suspicious eyes and great nose. His wife, according to him, is a schizophrenic but admits that he too is considered crazy. Twice married, he has whole bunch of children. But somehow he does not seem to be truly related to them, he is all alone and miserable because there is a persistent cry coming out from his deepest self 'I want' which he is not able to satisfy. Restless and conflict-torn he leaves everything like an ascetic and goes into the heart of dark Africa. There is a lot of physical suffering, hardships and obstacles but he moves on and on, inspired by his inner urge. He suffers humiliation with Arnewi people. With Warriri people he feels he has better luck and he becomes their Rain King. He learns to confront death which is the key to a restful life. Somehow he disentangles himself from this doomed position (becoming a king he was bound to be hanged when sexually not so potent) and comes back to America and to his family with a new enthusiasm. He does not want to die now but loves life, not only his own, but other's as well, and therefore decides to enter medical school, however late it might have been.

Bellow has made Henderson appear often larger than life, a mythical figure, who embodies many of the fears and aspirations of a whole generation of Americans. The surface of the book is comic and the centre is deeply serious. Henderson is a kind of fool but persists enough in his folly to reach the threshold of wisdom. His search is rendered half seriously and half mockingly. Yet it is capable of touching our hearts with its sincerity of emotion. Africa is the metaphor for one's own deeper, darker, dreaded self, Bellow wants to impress upon us that without facing and finding our own little known depths we cannot think of salvation. Secondly, only he who knows how to die will be able to know how to live, what to do with life.

His next novel *Herzog* (1964) is on the theme of reconciliation of the self with society. It takes intellectual sophistication at its heart which alienates an individual from others. It demonstrates that the life of the mind can, in fact, be as important and exciting a source of creative vitality as the life of the grain. Bellow here excels himself by presenting not only the important but the curse and comedy of intense consciousness.

Herzog—a man, somewhat out of his mind, is a twice divorced husband, an affectionate but irresponsible father of two small children. He lives all alone, either in his country house at Berkshires or in New York. He had been a bad husband to Daisy his first wife and he is deceived and treated badly by his second wife Madeleine, who is years young to him. To his own parents he had been an ungrateful child, to his country, an indifferent citizen, to his brother and sisters affectionate but remote, with his friends an egoist love lazy, with brightness dull, with power passive, with his own soul evasive. His present occupation is to brood on his past life and to write letters to the people—related or unrelated to him—which are never posted. He is not stable, cannot decide world wisely. Hurt or rather injured badly by his wife and his only close friend he is intent upon analyzing his wound. On the spur of the moment he flies to Chicago, taking his late father's revolver he goes to the residence of his ex-wife. But when he sees his wife's lover playing with his daughter June affectionately he is relieved and comes back. He is arrested and interrogated for some time for carrying a deadly weapon loaded but acquitted. But his facing his wife at the police station, again gives him peace of mind and in the end we find him resting peacefully in his country house.

Herzog's response to life is an intellectual one, and he feels himself called upon to give opinion on different problems of life faced by the human race but reaches nowhere. At last, he comes to realize that there is something important which cannot be explained, the reason and the rational approach leads you nowhere. Consequently, he withdraws himself from all mental activity and finds peace and even joy in his early human status.

Bellow's *Mr. Sammler's Planet* (1970) is another timely based theme novel. The action takes place on a day, night and the next day in April 1969 in New York City, just before the first Apollo lunar landing. Mr. Arter Sammler is a displaced person—that perhaps we all are—who is living on the charity of arch, kind, distant relative. The ugliness, madness, violence and obscenity of the 20th century life are exposed to the full.

Mr. Sammler, a Polish Jew has surprisingly survived the bloody melodrama. He was shot at and thought to be dead but somehow remains alive and creeps out of the grave. Wifeless and homeless he has only one daughter who according to him is not quite sane. One eyed Sammler, in this old age is playing the role of a friend, philosopher and guide to the younger generation, but at times he is disgusted with this rootless revolting and protesting generation. He is an author as well and his daughter wants him to write his memoirs. Shula Slava, his daughter, steals the manuscript of Dr. Govinda Lal, an Indian Scientist and as a result a meeting takes place between these two learned men. Ironically enough, Dr. Lal pleads for lunar landing but Sammler, representative of a materialistic nation does not approve of it. Sammler is late in reaching the hospital and his nephew and benefactor Dr. Gurumer is dead. He prays to God standing near his dead body.

Thus, Mr. Sammler, whose life has been a difficult one, who is surrounded by hairy deity, rude, vulgar, mad people, but who still refuses to be disappointed, seems to say that losing battles may be the order of the day and Mr. Sammler's planet may be a poor worn out earth—repellent and nauseating at times—he will still be here. He certainly brushes a way the idea of migrating to moon. He would rather search peace of mind here only, in his own being.

His next novel *Humboldt's Gift* (1976) is on the theme of ill treatment meted out to authors and thinkers by the society. The vanities, deceptions and manipulations of these intellectuals are also exposed. But the novel concerns itself with the moral and spiritual barrenness which surrounds a human being in this world, and perverted sexual attitude, rebellion and protest, which empties life out of any value.

Charlie Citrine is a close associate of Humboldt who is a writer and a famous man holding a high academic post. Due to unfavourable circumstances and his own jealous nature and unsteady mind he starts starving and is completely forgotten by the world. Charlie Citrine remembers him, wants to help him but his help is declined and he is thought to be an enemy. However, he comes to see his will after his death which contains one script of a scenario which is sold for a considerable sum of money. He is reburied now according to his wish. Citrine's own brother, a rich man, is going for a major operation but instead of thinking over life and death he has some gorgeous piece of property in his mind, because man had become materialistic to the core. Charlie wants to console him that death is only the end of the known thing. It cannot kill such a wonderful thing.

Thus *Humboldt's Gift* establishes that man can save himself with the idea of the immortality of the soul only. Faith is the only alternative to the path of salvation. One has to leave behind everything including one's own separate identity, ego, pride and the desire to be someone in particular.

Bellow's next novel *The Dean's December* (1982) is a tale of two cities. The protagonist, Albert Corde, a newspaperman becomes a professor of journalism and subsequently dean of students in an unnamed Chicago College. As dean, he has embroiled himself in controversy by writing a series of articles indicting Chicago for its racism, its clubhouse politics and its lack of what he calls 'moral initiative'. He presses for the conviction of a black man who murdered a white student of the college. He is dear neither to the college provost nor to the young liberals on the campus. So, he jeopardizes his professional standing as both journalist and college official by his impulse to take absolute moral readings.

The dean is geographically, if not mentally, distanced from the Chicago fray when he and his wife Minna spend the month of December in Bucharest visiting her dying mother, the distinguished psychiat Valeria Raresh. From the outset of their stay, they find that a Rumanian official obstructs their visits to the dying woman, apparently because of Valeria's history of disdain for the Socialist government. Thirty years earlier she had fallen into disfavour as minister of health; officially exonerated years later, she had declined to rejoin the party. The government officials respect Minna's international standing as an astrophysicist, but she had defected from Rumania twenty years earlier while studying in the west, and they are not disposed to overlook Valeria's behaviour for her sake. Indeed, because she did not formally renounce Romanian citizenship when she became a citizen of the United States, she is arguably subject to Romanian authority—a situation that worries Corde. Incautious conversation must never be indulged in her mother's wiretapped apartment, he warns, and he is anxious that they leave as soon as possible after Valerias death on Christmas eve.

Dewey Spangler, a childhood friend of Corde, happens to be in Bucharest when Valeria dies, and Corde confides in him imprudently so, because Spangler is an international journalist who fancies himself a Walter Lippmann. Upon the dean's return to America he is embarrassed to find he has given Spangler an interview and is the subject of one of his columns. Insidiously, the column mimics the dean's articles about Chicago in tone and style, and pseudo-analytical eloquence Spangler concludes that Corde possesses "earnestness too great for his capacities". So damning is the indictment and so dismissive Spangler's suggestion that Corde went into shock when he glimpsed the world outside academe that Corde feels his professional credibility destroyed, at least in moral matters. He resigns deanship immediately, intending to write further articles but no longer attracted to controversy. The novel ends with him accompanying Minna to the Mount Palomar observatory and travelling with her in a lift attached to one of the dome's structural arches, following its curve to the apex, and then returning again to the floor. Aware of this obvious analogy to his fall from moral authority, he reflects that it is not the extraordinary cold of the observatory that he minds so much as the coming down again.

Bellow's *More Die of Heartbreak* (1987) centres on a relationship between two men: thirty five year old Kenneth Trachtenberg, who narrates the story in somewhat slapdash fashion, and Benn Crader, who is his maternal uncle. Raised in France by American expatriate parents, Kenneth has returned to the American Midwest and taken a position teaching Russian literature at the same "Rustbelt" university that employs his uncle. Benn is a world-class botanist a specialist in the anatomy and morphology of plants—but Kenneth sees him fondly as "one of those old-time Kansas banks that any punk robber could knock over". A widower, Benn proves especially vulnerable to women. Profoundly distressing to him is the memory of neighbour named Della Bedell, who said a manic claim to his sexual favours and whom he evaded by arranging a lecture tour in Brazil. In the wake of her death shortly afterward, a newspaper asks for a statement about the effects of nuclear radiation and Benn makes the remark that gives the novel its title: "It's terribly serious, of course, but I think more people die of heartbreak than of radiation".

Of more concern to Kenneth than the heartbreak of Mrs. Bedell is his uncle's subsequent marriage to a society beauty named Matilda Lyamon, twenty years his junior and the daughter of a wealthy gynecologist. It develops that the entrepreneurial Lyamons plan to make Benn a millionaire several times over by reversing a crooked real-estate deal in which he and his sister had been victimized years before by their uncle Harold Vilitzer, an old-style ward boss said to have once cracked a man's head in a vise. Benn has no sympathy with the scheme. Not really wanting the money and with no taste for family blood, he fails to take action against his uncle and departs secretly for the North Pole with an international team of scientists, leaving Matilda to have their marriage annulled if she chooses. His escape from Mrs. Bedell is the pattern of his escape from Matilda's immediate predecessor, Caroline Bunge, whom he abandoned almost at the altar. Who was it, Benn asks his nephew in parting, who described him as "a phoenix who runs with arsonists"?

As Kenneth counsels his uncle and listens to his problems often in that order, he suffers vaguely analogous difficulties. Treckie Sterling, the mother of his daughter but not his wife, as he frequently reminds us, has moved to Oregon, where she is cohabiting with a burly ski instructor. In the manner of his uncle's women, Treckie's mother subsequently makes a bid to marry Kenneth. "Not for me, thank you ma'am", Kenneth mutters, but Mrs. Sterling's less than—sterling proposition inspires him to visit Treckie and his young daughter. On his return to the Midwest, he turns with increasing affection to a former student named Dita, no beauty or socialite, but a gentle woman. The novel's imagery of fire and polar ice belongs to Benn's emotional life, not to Kenneth's, but Kenneth is, to some extent, a phoenix like his uncle, and his heart experiences a modest resurrection at the end.

In this way, Bellow has restlessly sought a new milieu, original structures or plots, various kinds of characters, different styles, yet the main concern remains the same and that is to depict the conflict between man's spiritual and his experience of life of the society, of the world and even of the universe. It is a society in which a sensitive and vulnerable person who has a deeper need to fulfil, a higher urge to satisfy, can never feel at home. Neither can he have a colony of the spirit he will have to dwell apart, if he cannot sell himself out to compromises, he sees daily around him.

The dominant mood in nineteen thirties and nineteen forties in society as well as in literature, in the sense of separate and unconciliating identity, it was not only due to the fact that the individual found it difficult to communicate with his fellows, but also because he had lost touch with an over-reaching definition of himself. Marcus Klein puts it thus "it is not only the chaos of the society they are afraid of, but the individual personality is also filled with its own chaos".[33] Nearly every artist of these two decades has directly or indirectly addressed himself to this central problem bringing to it his own interpretations. "Bellow also expresses the sense of alienation common enough in our time",[34] says Robert Gorham Davis.

I feel that almost all heroes of Bellow's novels give the air of brooding apart. They do not seem to belong to this world, they are all outsiders and what the sociologist would call—Marginal men. They are all conscious of being in an interim situation. Their deepest feeling is a sense of displacement, whether rich or poor, young or old, intellectuals or otherwise. They may be living in a six-sided-box type room, or in a hotel or in some city-apartment or in some secluded country house, they are always out of place. They have no roots, no contacts, not at ease with anyone except their own selves. They lead solitary, loveless life and live like exiles from the society. It does not make any difference even if they are married, having children, and even having mistresses. They derived their moral energy from some internal source of which their fellow travellers in life are somewhat ignorant. Sometimes they even make the confident reader uncomfortable by dramatizing for him the painful struggle of an alienated existence.

Some critics like John Jacob Clayton and Richard Poirior feel that in spite of Bellow's strong desire to affirm life, his heroes are all alienated because of the fact that he is himself an alienated being and a masochist. By being a typical product of his social atmosphere and literary background, and being a Jew who is a typical example of an alienatee for centuries, he cannot be other than what he is. In terms of family and childhood background, Bellow's is a case of multiple dislocations. Robert Gorham Davis says, "Without knowing it Bellow is far more alienated than Mailer".[35] Jacob Clayton finds that "the defender of the human dignity and freedom of the individual, he who affirms humanity, is none other than alienate".[36]

However, I have an entirely different view and disagree with these critical statements. I find another reason for Bellow's heroes to be alienated from society and everything in general. Although I am concerned with the problem of humanism in the novels of Bellow only, and not more than that I put forward the point that Bellow's protagonists alienate themselves purposely. Their invariable loneliness is felt by them and by us, not only as a function of urban life and the atomization of culture but as something willed. All his heroes are under immense load and pressure, which they do not and cannot share with anyone else. They are alone and fragmented because they continue posing questions which are of scant interest.

References

1. Saul Bellow, *To Jerusalem and Back* (Penguin Books, 1977), p. 111.
2. Philip P. Mason, "Working in America in Issues and Themes: Essays", *American History and Civilization* (American Association for State and Local History, 1975), p. 129.
3. Rod W. Horton and Herbert W. Edwards, *Background of American Literary Thought*, 2nd edn. (Meredith Publishing Company, 1969), p. 293.
4. Laurence Veysey, "Growing up in America in Issues and Themes: Essays", *American History and Civilization* (American Association for State and Local History, 1975), p. 245.
5. *Ibid.*
6. Herbert J. Muller, *Modern Fiction: A Study of Values* (New York, 1937), p. 3.
7. Donald Heiney and Lenthiel H. Downs, *Recent American Literature* (Barrons Educational Series, 1971), p. 15.
8. Leslie A. Fielder, "The Jewish Writer and the English Literary Tradition", *Commentary* (October, 1949), p. 14.
9. Saul Bellow, "Where Do We Go from Here: The Future of Fiction" in *Saul Bellow and the Critics,* ed. Irving Malin (New York University Press, 1967), p. 214.
10. Maxwell Geismar, "Saul Bellow: Novelist of the Intellecluals", *American Modern from Rebellion to Conformity* (Hill and Wang, New York, 1965), p. 217.
11. Helen Weinberg, *The New Novel in America: The Kafkan Made in Contemporary Fiction* (Cornell University Press, Ithaca and London, 1970), p. XI.
12. Jonalhan Baumback, *The Landscape of Nightmare: Studies in Contemporary Novel* (New York University Press, 1965), pp. 35-36.

13. Robert Gorham Davis, "The American Individualist Tradition: Bellow and Styron", *The Creative Present,* ed. Nona (Balakian and Company, Gardencity, New York, 1963), p. 112.

14. Irving Malin, *Saul Bellow's Fiction* (Carbondale, Southern Illinois University Press, 1969), Preface.

15. Ihab Hassan, *Radical Innocence: Studies in Contemporary American Novel* (Princeton University Press, 1961), p. 303.

16. Marcus Klein, "A Discipline of Nobility", *After Alienation: American Novel in Mid-Century* (New York, 1965), p. 30.

17. Ihab Hassan, *Radical Innocence: Studies in Contemporary American Novel* (Princeton University Press, 1961), p. 303.

18. Peter M. Axthelm, *The Modern Confessional Novel* (New Heaven and London Yale University Press, 1969), p. 23.

19. Helen Weinberg, "Kafka and Bellow", *The New Novel in America* (Ithaca & London, Cornell University Press, 1970), p. 36.

20. Tony Tanner, *Saul Bellow* (Olive and Byed, Edinburgh, 1965), p. 9.

21. Theodore J. Ross, "Notes on Saul Bellow", *Chicago Jewish Forum* 18 (April, 1962), p. 24.

22. Henry Fairle, "Epistle of a Gentile to Saul Bellow", *The New Republic* (February 5, 1977), p. 19.

23. Saul Bellow, *Jerusalem Post Weekly*, 507 (July 13, 1970), p. 14.

24. *Ibid.*

25. Maxwell Geiswar, "Saul Bellow: Novelist of the Intellectuals" in *American Moderns from Rebellion to Conformity* (Hill and Wang, New York, 1965), p. 216.

26. Alfred Kazin, *Bright Book of Life: American Novelists and Story Tellers From Hemingway to Mailer* (New Delhi, Allied Publishers, 1973), p. 130.

27. Saul Bellow, *To Jerusalem and Back* (Penguin Books, 1977), p. 14.

28. Alfred Kazin, *Contemporaries* (Boston and Toronto, Little Brown and Company, 1958), p. 217.

29. Saul Bellow, "Where Do We Go from Here: The Future of Fiction", *Critical Approaches to Fiction,* ed. Shiv K. Kumar (USA, McGraw Hill Book Company, 1968), p. 11.

30. Maxwell Geismar, "Saul Bellow: Novelist of the Intellectuals" in *American Moderns from Rebellion to Conformity* (Hill and Wang New York, 1965), p. 212.
31. Saul Bellow, *Dangling Man* (Harmondsworth, 1985), p. 10.
32. Jack Ludwig, *Recent American Novelists* (University of Minnesota Pamphlets, 1962), p. 10.
33. Marcus Klein, *After Alienation: American Novel in Mid-Century* (Free Port New York, Books for Library Press, 1965), p. 46.
34. Robert Gorham Davis, "The American Individualist Tradition", *The Creative Present,* eds. Nona Balakian and C. Simons (Garden City, NY, Doubleday and Company, 1965), p. 46.
35. Richard Poirier, "Herzog or Bellow in Trouble", *Saul Bellow, Twentieth Century Views,* ed. Earl Rovit (Princeton Hall, N.J., 1975), p. 81.
36. John J. Clayton, *Saul Bellow: In Denfense of Man* (Bloomington's Indiana University Press, 1968), p. 64.

2

Dangling Man

Dangling Man (1944) is the journal of a young man named Joseph, who lives with his wife in a Chicago rooming house while waiting to be called up for services in World War II. A Canadian citizen who has been living in America for eighteen years at the beginning of the novel, he has received an induction notice from the United States Army, quit his job with the Inter-American Travel Bureau, passed his physical, and has been accepted for military service. At that point his status as a friendly alien results in a bureaucratic tangle that delays his official induction and leaves him 'dangling' neither a functioning civilian nor an official soldier. He spends his days in bed, reading newspapers and magazines, or wandering the streets on improvised errands. After seven months of such indolence, he begins to keep the journal that is the novel. He maintains it with almost daily entries from Dec 15, 1942 to April 9, 1943.

Because Joseph is simply enduring life while awaiting induction and because his life is generally uneventful, the novel has little plotting in the conventional sense of the term 'Fairly quiet day', he observes sardonically in an entry for Jan 16, for his days are so predictably quiet that he has begun to mark time by such mnemonics as 'the day I asked for second cup of coffee' or 'the day the waitress refused to take back the burned toast'. One of the symptoms of Joseph's malaise is a tendency to crap on the deficiencies of those around him. His wife Iva is glad to support him during the period of waiting and hopes he will use the leisure to finish a series of essays he has started to write on the philosophers of the Enlightenment, but she 'has a way about her that discourages talk' and is accused of being more interested in fashion magazines than in his insights. Her mother Mrs. Almstadt is a vague and foolish woman who dresses her bed ridden husband with preposterous gentility 'like a mandarin' Joseph scoffs. His brother Amos is spurned as a war profiteer who tries not to disapprove of Joseph too openly, and his niece Etta is a thoroughly disagreeable who hates her uncle Joseph without apology or reserve.

In Joseph's estimation his friends and acquaintances are as generally inappreciable a lot as his family. His friend Morris Abt is a self-conscious intellectual 'Continually in need of being consequential'. His friend Alf Steidler is a cultural drop out who expects to be thought interesting for his indolence. A man named Myron Adler is dismissed as one who 'has learned, like so many others, to prize convenience...to be accommodating', and an artist named John Pearl is patronized as one whose respect for the imagination 'confers a sort of life on him'. A senile old man named Vanaker haunts the corridors and toilets of the rooming house, driving Joseph paroxysms of indignation, and a maid named Marie dares to smoke while cleaning Joseph's room—which he thinks a bold-faced freedom and a personal interest.

But the deeper symptom of Joseph's malaise is an absorption in his own states of mind so intense that it seems a voyeurism turned inward. The swings of his emotional life and the metaphysical implications of his experience obsess him life contemporary furies, and the war itself is unnoticed as he attends relentlessly to minutiae of daily experience. Indolence gradually gives way to irritation, to violence and finally Joseph can control his furies no longer. After a wild public outburst over Vanaker's failure to close a bathroom door, he is asked to leave the boarding house. Deciding then that it was impossible to resist any longer, he makes a decision to surrender and asks the draft board to place his name at the top of induction list. Two weeks later, he observes his last day as a civilian and ends the novel with a cheer half ironic, half sincere for his loss of freedom:

> Hurray for regular hours.
> And for the supervision of the spirit
> Long live regimentation!

Dangling Man is supposed to be an infinitely complex examination of a contemporary Robinson Crusoe Joseph, the hero of the novel considers himself as 'a moral casualty of the war'. He snaps at friends, quarrels with his near relatives, clamps on his wife. The very presence of others is loathsome to him. Not only this, but he isolates himself from the 'old Joseph'. Existing in an ever narrowing circle, by the middle of the novel he is completely solitary except an alter ego, the second self. He walks unfamiliar faces and goes on changing his restaurants very often in order to avoid any friendliness. He has stopped going to any party or any friend, his wife is out of his inner world, he has served his connection with his mistress Kitty Damler and frequently quarrels with other tenants. His brother Amos is surprised at his behaviour with his daughter. Disgusted with himself and the surroundings eventually he does begin to lose all sense of time and this distorted time sense indicates an attitude of difference to the physical surrounding and withdrawal from temporal existence in the world, into more speculative and timeless self awareness. He addresses himself to the questions which are counter to the rules of the game we play in culture.

In *Dangling Man*, Bellow presents the trauma and trouble of his young hero, Joseph who has resigned his job in the travel agency to join the army. A Jewish humanist intellectual, Joseph represents the agony of not merely a Jewish-American, but also that of a modern man himself, who cannot evade the prevailing conditions in the present century. Waiting to be drafted, Joseph has to undergo the torturing effect of modern bureaucracy:

> ...a trivial seeming thing, a sort of bureaucratic comedy trimmed out in red tape. (*DM*, p. 8)

"He is made to shuttle back and forth as a result of the red tapism" (pp. 8-9). This forces him to dangle and his dangling state has its inevitable effect on his mental world.

> There is nothing to do but wait, or dangle, and grow more and more dispirited. It is perfectly clear to me that I am deteriorating, storing bitterness and in spite of which eat like acids at my endowment of generosity and goodwill. But the seven months delay is only one of the sources of my harassment. (p. 10)

This makes him confined to his room and generally he grows isolated from the outside world. His self gets imprisoned in his room. Like Dostoevsky's underground man, Joseph becomes motionless and "grows rooted to my chair" (p. 10). He is thrown back upon himself and finds his existence without essence in a hostile world. The quest goes inward from social life into his private rooms where "...I am very much alone. I sit idle in my room anticipating the minor crises of the day..." (p. 9). His world is confined to the four walls of his room. Although his dangling state originates from his awaiting to be drafted, there are convincing evidences in his entries to the journal that his dangling is not only between the civil and military life, but the entries of his first hero, Bellow sketches his ideas on self and the world in the present day context to be developed further in his later novels.

During the process of induction into the army, he has to encounter the repeated enquiries regarding his identity. This stimulates his sense of personal identity. Without any job he has no status and is trash in the eye of the society in which he lives. Society would not accord him a personal identity and attach importance to a person like him. Even his maid Marie smokes before him and he ignores his identity.

> The maid knocks and pushes open the door. She has a cigarette in her mouth. I think I am the only one before whom she dares smoke. She recognizes that I am of no importance. (p. 12)

His mother-in-law speaks of him unfavourably and offers him a glass of orange juice in which he discovers a brown feather floating. He pours the juice down the drain (p. 19). This is a direct assault to his sensitivity and makes him more spiteful. Likewise, when his ex-communist friend Jimmy Burns altogether ignores him in the restaurant. Joseph is caught by fury and demands his due recognition.

> I have a right to be spoken to. I it's the most elementary things in the world. Simply that I insist on it. (p. 27)

The bank manager refuses to encash a cheque, as he fails to satisfy him of his identity.

The above mentioned instances make it clear that without any position, society is reluctant to accord a sense of dignity to Joseph as a human being. Joseph, "the creature of plans", who wants to live as "good man", is thus thrust into self-imprisonment. His questioning self comes into conflict with the outside world. As a result, his relationship with his family, friends and acquaintances deteriorates and becomes a strenuous one. While he cannot adjust himself with their version of reality, he cannot convert them into his own ideas either.

> What he wanted was 'a colony of the spirit', or a group whose covenants forbade spite, bloodiness and cruelty.... The world was crude and it was dangerous and if no measures were taken, existence could indeed become—in Hobbes's phrase, which had long ago lodged in Joseph's mind—'nasty, brutish and short'. It need not become so if a number of other would combine to defend themselves against danger and crudity. (p. 32)

But Joseph cannot find 'those others' to join him in his attempt to save life from becoming 'nasty, brutish and short'. Rather majority around him including his brother Amos appear before him, as what a later Bellow's hero would term as 'Reality instructors'. These reality instructors want to teach Joseph the ways of the world and to submit to the group values.

His brother Amos epitomizes the current of the present day world that attaches much importance to money. Money is the measuring stick of success and status in the present day world. Amos in fact has been disapproved of Joseph's choice of every step in his career, simply because Joseph attaches less value to money. Amos who wears a dozen of shoes a year cannot believe that "it is possible for a member of his family to live on so little" (p. 49). It is because of the influence of money that his daughter has grown up to be a reckless girl, who would not show even the minimum sense of courtesy and addresses Joseph by his first name. As it will be revealed further in his later novels, Bellow's heroes are not interested in making money. While most of them remain short of it, they come to view it as something trivial. Considering himself to be a "moral casualty of war" (p. 14). Joseph makes it clear that he does not want to build up his future through war. More than this, the present crisis makes Joseph aware that there is hardly any personal future left for individual. He tells Amos:

> There are many people, hundreds of thousands, who have had to give up all thought of future. There is no personal future any more. That's why I can only laugh at you when you tell me to look out for my future in the Army, in that tragedy, I wouldn't stake a pin on my future. (p. 54)

Even when living at the minimum, Joseph's sense of self-respect forbids him to accept the hundred dollar offered by his rich brother.

The money centred hollowness of city life naturally fails to satisfy the inner self of Joseph. Rather it creates chaos and increases his pain. His conversation with Amos and a few of his friends make it amply evident that there had been a persistent longing in Joseph of a personal destiny. But society at large does not promote his quest for identity. As such he too fails to adjust himself with the group life. The chaos of a modern but hollow culture disturbs his inner peace of mind. He grows increasingly harsh, bitter and quarrelsome. His rebellious behaviour may be interpreted as a part of his identity seeking. He becomes rebellious, because the harsher and dehumanized out world would not allow him to assert his individuality. The reality as it exists, insists that man submits to group values without attaching any importance to the need of his inner self. Such a collision threatens his integrity and hence the clash resulting in his isolation.

It is while remaining in his isolation that Bellow works out miraculous discovery of the part of his intellectual hero. Although Joseph suffers from a feeling of strangeness, of not quite belonging to the world, of lying under cloud, he has nevertheless a firm faith in the meaning and possibility of life. Life for him is beauty:

> In a sense everything is good because it exists. Or, good or not good, it exists, it is ineffable, and for that reason, marvelous. (p. 24)

This faith is constant with him and therefore he rejects alienation as a fool's plea, and also rejects the idea of worshipping anti-life as suggested by Tu As Raison Aussi. What makes him temporarily isolated is the fact that as the world around him would not allow him to assert his individuality in order to realize its full potentiality, he is confused and seeks in his inner mind the answer to the question of his troubled self and creates a world of his own, "But I must know what I myself am" (p. 99). Introspective by nature, he is given to more intros, and tries to acquire wholeness, despite his being aware that he cannot attain it without aid:

> And was I to become this whole man alone, without aid? I was too weak for it. I did not command the will. Then in what quarter should I look for help, where was the power? (pp. 55-56)

At the first instance, his pride prevents him to look forward to God for the aid he is in need of finding no way out to his dangling state, suffering becomes his lot. In a Bellow novel the suffering of the hero positively contributes to his affirmative attitude toward life Bellow dramatizes the clash between the "yes" and "no" to life through the suffering of his hero:

> Great pressure is brought to bear to make us undervalue ourselves. On the other hand, civilization teaches that each of us is an inestimable prize. There are, then, these two preparations. One for life and the other for death. Therefore we value and are ashamed to value ourselves, are hard boiled. (p. 98)

When Mr. Fanzel, the tailor, and Joseph's own brother Amos are profiting by the war like other, Joseph is concerned with the questions like 'how a good man should live'. It is this questing spirit engaged in finding answers to difficult questions which is at the root of his alienation. He is busy in finding a separate identity in a society which takes human beings as functions only. A pattern of continued failure to reconcile satisfactorily the ideal with the real that leads to Joseph's ever increasing alienation. He alienates himself because he feels he cannot live a purposeless, a moralless and useless life like others, material prosperity which counts so much for other is insignificant to him. He is bent upon finding a meaning behind this apparent life.

It goes without saying that the Bellow's hero would choose life and not death on what he persists is that life be based on values, which he cannot discover in the world around him. As hinted earlier, even waiting for the induction, he has his genuine feeling for the common humanity.

Joseph wants to retain the basic innocence of his heart. Unlike his brother or the tailor Mr. Fanzel, he chooses not to consume the benefits of war. If it does express a sense of liking to be a 'victim' on the part of the Bellow hero, it equally brings to the forefront his primal innocence. Joseph comes to embody the human element against the dehumanized world.

> Myself, I would rather die in the war than consume its benefits. When I am called, I shall go and make no protest. And of course I hope to survive. But I would rather be a victim than a beneficiary. (p. 69)

He is preparing himself to join the army. It is the choice offered to him at a time when "personal choice doesn't count for much these days". He knows that he must join the war, because choice is limited and everyone accepts what is offered to him:

> Yes I shall shoot, I shall take lives; I shall be shot at, and my life may be taken. Certain blood will be given for half certain reasons as in all wars. Some how I cannot regard it was wrong against myself. (p. 69)

It is significant here that waiting to be drafted and preparing himself to take lives, he wants to survive. More than this he wants to be drafted and preparing himself to take lives, he wants "to survive" and at the same time he wants "to be a member of the Army, but not a part of it". His inner world begins to be illuminated with his growing awareness. This awareness in turn teaches him to acknowledge and accept the limitations of the self:

> I know that I shall have to settle for very little, very little. That is, I shall have to accept very little.... (p. 103)

Bellow juxtaposes the sense of salvation of the human self with a sense of history and hints at the potentialities of the self under changed circumstances:

> Six hundred years ago, a man was what he was born to be. Satan and Church, representing God, did battle over him. He, by the reason of his choice, partially decided the outcome. But whether after life, he went to hell or heaven, his place among other men was given. It couldn't be contested. But since, the stage has been reset and human beings only walk on it, and under this revision, we have, instead history to answer to. We were important enough then for our souls to be fought over. Now each of us is responsible for his own salvation, which is in his greatness. (p. 73)

Joseph's belief in the possibility of this salvation prompts him to negate anti-life. He tells the Spirit of Alternatives:

> ...there are no values outside life. There is nothing outside life. (p. 137)

And human life means sharing with human beings. The following utterances make it amply evident that Joseph has all along within him a longing to join the community life:

> I would be denying my inmost feeling if I said I wanted to be by-passed and spared from knowing what the rest of my generation is undergoing. I don't want to be hamped protectively over my life. I am neither so corrupt, nor so hard-boiled that I can savor my life only when it is in danger of extinction. But on the other hand,

> its value here in this room is decreasing day by day. Soon it may become distasteful to me. (p. 138)

What Bellow does want to vindicate is that absence of communication does not lend meaning to life. Existence without communication with other human beings is short of love. One can earn dignity for his self only in communion with others. Striving for freedom, Joseph in his room soon learns that a good man ought to live in company of others:

> And goodness is achieved not in a vacuum, but in the company of other men, attended by love. I, in this room, separate, alienated, distrustful, find in my jail. My perspectives end in the walls. Nothing of the future comes to me. Only the past, in its shabbiness and innocence. (p. 75)

In order to make one's life meaningful and to continue it in order, one must establish a relationship with others. There is no doubt that this relationship is to be based on love. An individual can attain wholeness only by accepting the limitations of the self: "True, that man's life is limited by death and he must accept death" (p. 101). Even accepting his death a man can have meaningful rapport with fellow human beings. Only then his life becomes glory and beauty. Contrary to this when one invites death, he negates a power that lies within him. This is the power of choice. Continuation of life means continuation of choice that may in time enable a man to realize his potentialities. Death curtails the power of choice and thereby deprives a man of his possibilities. But so long a man is alive he is the master of himself within imposed limitations:

> ...continued life means expectation. Death is the abolition of choice. The more choice is limited, the closer we are to death. The greatest cruelty is to curtail expectations without taking away life completely. A life term in prison is life that so is citizenship in some countries. The best solution would be to live as if the ordinary expectations had not been removed, not from day to day, blindly. But that requires immense self-mastery. (p. 122)

The "immense self mastery" which Bellow talks of is nothing but the courage, that is required to affirm life in the face of nihilism. While he remains dangling and alienated, Joseph earns more of this mastery in the process of his rebirth. Joseph declares that judgment is the second to wonder and his intellect would not alone have been enough to create the state of illumination in his world, that urges him to continue life in all its limitations. It is implied that these limitations render discipline to human life. Not only the army life, but life in general too has its order that makes it beautiful. And discipline implies submission. As Joseph's friend Robbie Still-man says:

> Army life...is not hard when you are accustomed yourself to discipline. You have to learn to submit. (p. 125)

Man's own 'ideal constructions' seldom provide the sense of destiny sought for. At the same time it is through the creation of an 'ideal realm' of one's own however untenable it may be and however one be tenacious to it, that one can become aware of the 'real' one. Joseph's yearning to join humanity teaches him what the highest 'ideal construction' is:

> ...the highest ideal construction is the one that unlocks the imprisoning self. (p. 127)

No one can attain freedom unless and until his imprisoned self is released. And his self will be free, only when he learns to share his fate with other human beings. Paradoxically, it is during his alienated state that Joseph falls back on his own inner resources and discovers certain enduring truths which cause reawakening in his inner self. By making his hero move inward, Bellow performs a two-fold purpose. He makes his hero alienated to discover the meaninglessness of alienation. It is his alienation that Joseph comes to realize certain truths which would finally cure the malaise of his tormented self. Again it is these truths which make him realize that human life has no meaning in isolation. It can achieve wholeness only in meaning participation in community life. This reawakening causes a transformation in Joseph who now ceases to hanker after his narrower sense of 'personal destiny' and becomes aware of a large body. His agony is cooling down as his self is going to merge itself with the greater humanity. Only in such merger, the self can attain its true dignity, and therefore, freedom:

> The quest, I am begging to think, whether it be for money, for notoriety, reputation, increase of pride, whether it leads to thievery slaughter, sacrifice, the quest is the one and the same. All the striving is for one end. I do not entirely understand this impulse. But it seems to me that its final end is the desire for pure freedom. We are all drawn towards the same craters of the spirit to know what we are and what we are for, to know our purpose, to seek grace. And if the quest is the same, the differences in our personal histories, which hither to meant so much to us, become of minor importance. (pp. 127-28)

In his constant endeavour to define the true stature of a man in the present century, Bellow here brings his 'humanist ideal' to the surface and hints that led by mere narrower self interests, one does not and cannot earn the ability to join the common humanity to make ones' life meaningful.

Joseph eases his mind and when he views the war in a larger perspective, he considers it as nothing but an 'incident', something comparable to his childhood diseases which he fought 'to become Joseph'. His desire to join the war implies submission and it is in this submissive state that Joseph now wants to continue his search for freedom:

> ...the self that we must govern. Chance must not govern it, incident must not govern it. It is our humanity that we are responsible for it, our dignity, our freedom.... I cannot ask to be immune from the war. I have to take my risks for survival as I did, formerly, against childhood diseases and all the dangers and accidents through which I nevertheless managed to become Joseph. (p. 139)

Joseph by now has learnt that his search would continue so long as he remains alive. He has learnt to cope with reality as it exists:

> The war can destroy me physically. That it can do. But so can bacteria. I must be concerned with them naturally; I must take account of them. They can obliterate me. But as long as I am alive, I must follow my destiny in spite of them. (p. 140)

Bellow's solutions are tentative. Although Joseph vows to continue his search till his death, Bellow's young hero cannot answer the question asked by the spirit of Alternatives, as to whether he has a separate destiny as yet. His answer is, "I'm not ready to answer. I have nothing to say to that now" (p. 140). In any case, the reawakening in his consciousness has taught him to submit:

> I believe I had known for sometime that the moment I had been waiting for had come, and that it was impossible to resist any longer. I must give myself up. (p. 152)

This kind of submission adds order and meaning to the individual self. Because by joining the army, symbolically Joseph joins humanity—the greater worlds, of which the individual self is only a tiny part:

> I had not done well alone. I doubted whether anyone could. To be pushed upon oneself entirely put the very facts of simple existence in doubt. Perhaps the war could teach me, by violence, what I had been unable to learn during those months in the room. Perhaps I could sound creation through other means, perhaps. But things were now out of my hands. The next move was the world's. I could not bring myself to regret it. (p. 158)

The sceptical note of the utterances implies that Bellow is yet to arrive at a definite point regarding the self-society dichotomy which he would further explore in his later novels. Joseph hands him over to the regular hours of the army. His last entry (9 April) notes a kind of accommodation, if not of total affirmation, "I am no longer to be held accountable for myself; I am grateful for that I am in other hands, relieved of self-determination, freedom cancelled" (p. 159).

Bellow's formulation of self and freedom in his first novel is thus ironic and ambiguous. Nonetheless, his purpose becomes very much explicit that a good man should live in the company of other men and this is possible through love. In fact, the meaning of human existence itself comes to be doubtful when lived alone. Vindicating his faith in the dignity and possibilities of the individual self, Bellow makes it clear that one must learn to exert one's choice in the face of the imposed limitations. By the kind of submission, as of Joseph, Bellow never intends to mean the loss of the self in the crowd. What does he intend is that such submission is necessary condition which enables the individual to discover him in his sub-angelic position, only when he can qualify himself to join and merge with the humanity itself. His self then acquires dignity and meaning.

Reference

Bellow, Saul, *Dangling Man* (Harmondsworth, 1985). Subsequent references in parentheses are to this edition.

3

The Victim

The Victim[1] (1947) is a story of Asa Leventhal, a middle-class New York Jew, and his ostensible victimization one summer in New York by a gentile named Kirby Allbee. A few years prior to the novel's beginning Leventhal had found himself out of work, and Allbee had secured him an interview with his employer—a publisher named Rudiger. The interview was not a success: Rudiger was inexplicably insulting; Leventhal was rude in return; and Allbee was dismissed from his own position a few days later. Leventhal went on to find employment with a publisher of trade journals named Beard, while Allbee slipped inexorably into poverty. At the beginning of *The Victim*, Allbee makes a surprise reappearance in Leventhal's life accuses him of deliberately having created the scene years before in retaliation for a casually anti-Semetic remark Allbee once made in his hearing. Allbee claims that the loss of his job led to an estrangement with his wife, ultimately to her death in a traffic accident and to his subsequent alcoholism as well. He expects from Leventhal nothing less than a fearful symmetry: a job interview with Leventhal's present employer.

When Leventhal denies he had deliberately created a problem for Allbee and refuses to arrange an interview with Beard, Allbee insulates himself into Leventhal's life. He spies on him, follows him about, takes up residence in his apartment, reads private love notes from Leventhal's wife Mary, who is temporarily helping her mother in Atlanta, dallies with a prostitute in Leventhal's bed and eventually puts his head into Leventhal's oven in a suicide attempt—at which point Leventhal firmly ejects Allbee from both his home and his life. In a final chapter of the novel, the two meet accidentally a few years later while entering a theatre, and Allbee talks vaguely about having come 'to terms with whoever runs things'. Leventhal demands suddenly, 'wait a minute, what's your idea of who runs things?' But Allbee has already disappeared into the crowd, and Bellow leaves the question hanging.

A second plot line in the novel concerns Leventhal's relationship to the family of his brother Max who has left his wife Elena and his two sons Philip and Mickey in Staten Island while working in Texas and searching there for suitable lodging. Leventhal voluntarily assumes responsibility for watching over the family when Mickey falls sick in Max's absence, although he is annoyed by Elena's slovenliness and irritated that Beard is not more understanding about his need for time off. Eventually Mickey dies, and Max without the two brothers reading a new level of understanding and respect for one another.

The plot of *The Victim* centres round the theme of guilt and responsibility. Its protagonist Asa Leventhal is uncertain of his position in order of things. The Betile Allbee arises from the crowd to accuse Leventhal for the loss of his job. The novel tells the tale of social responsibility enforced in a world where self-definition thrown upon the individual himself has become a hard task indeed. Throughout the novels, Leventhal is haunted by repulsive Allbee and forced to scrutinize the nature and degree of responsibility of one human being for another. Bellow shows that the only being exactly human can one ascertain the nature and degree of such responsibility for one's fellow beings.

To work out such a solution out of the much puzzling situation, Bellow strikes a note of balance by equating the Jew and the gentile. It is a world where no one has a secured place. Every one here feels displaced and insecured. Bellow creates in this novel a mood of containment and tension, which eventually helps Leventhal to remove his fear and imaginary doubt of 'persecution'. While educating Leventhal the lesson of responsibility, Allbee makes it clear that human beings must share mutual responsibility. Leventhal first tries to evade such a responsibility but gradually comes to acknowledge the lesson of Allbee and prepares himself to share the responsibility for the loss of Allbee's job. More than Allbee, it is the Jewish theatre critic, Schlossberg, who helps Leventhal to clear his hazy mind and to know the meaning of human life and what it means to be human.

The point already amplified earlier, here one needs only to point out that despite his being an editor of a trade journal, Leventhal cannot be said to be an intellectual at par with Joseph. The questioning nature—a recurring feature in a Bellow hero, is lacking in Leventhal. Notwithstanding this he is introspective and frequently given to reflection. It is true that Leventhal's fear of persecution is in the main an imaginary one. What Bellow aims at, through the entangle of Leventhal and Allbee, is to focus on the existential crisis, that has been the lost of a man in modern times. Bellow's idea of the dignity of self and meaning of life at present are mainly worked out through the character of Schlossberg, while Allbee too voices some of Bellow's ideas on the state of man in the present century. These affirmative ideas help to clear up Leventhal's consciousness which gradually discovers some principles in the scheme of things.

In one of the encounters in the process of educating Leventhal, Allbee hints at the position of man at present:

> The day of succeeding by your own efforts is past. Now it's all blind movement, vast movement and the individual is shuttled back and forth. He only thinks that he's the works. But that isn't the way it is groups; organizations succeed or fail, but not individuals any longer. (*V*, p. 62)

While Allbee's utterances reveal the growing meagreness of the self in the face of a giant civilization his words can also be taken to be the hints of limitations of the individual, which he must accept in order to lead life on decent terms. In the tune of Joseph Allbee says that man's power to shape his own destiny no longer rests with him. Rather people do have a destiny forced in them:

> I don't know how you look at it, but I take it for granted that we're not gods. We are only creatures, and the things, we sometimes think, are permanent, they aren't permanent. So one day we're like full bundles and the next we're wrapping-paper, blowing around the streets. (p. 67)

Although appearing to be very powerful, Allbee's remarks reveal that actually everyone has become an example of victimized humanity in a deterministic universe-demanded by external forces.

Whatever may be the intention of Allbee in revealing such ideas before Leventhal, the latter cannot readily agree that he has been solely responsible one for the Allbee's job. Nonetheless, Allbee's utterances do have one inevitable effect on Leventhal's consciousness which gets a jerk. In Bellow's novel, the ultimate revelation or truth must come from the hero's own inner resources. Leventhal too penetrates further and comes up with a greater revelation:

> But what were all the codes and rules...except an answer to our own nature. Would we have to be told "Love!" if we loved as we breathed? No, obviously. This was not to say that we didn't love but had to be assisted whenever the motor started missing. The peculiar thing struck him that everything else in the nature was bounded; trees, dogs, and ants didn't grow beyond a certain size. "But we"..."in all directions without any limit". (p. 70)

Such reflections of Leventhal are clear signs of his consciousness being illuminated and it is in this way that he will come to posses his exact human stature. Only then his self can attain its true dignity and he can have his identity as a human being.

Two things move together in Leventhal. First, there is a growing awareness of what it means to be human and second his readiness for the acceptance of responsibility for another human being. As his friend Harkavy tells him:

> I have to take myself as I am or push off. I am all I have in this world. And with all my shortcomings my life is precious to me. My heart doesn't sink. Experience has taught me to expect this once in a while. But you're so upset when somebody doesn't like you, or say this or that about you. A little independence, boy, it's a weakness, positively. (p. 76)

Time becomes the best healer of Leventhal. His weakness becomes to lessen and his eyes are opened up toward some deeper truths. He comes to take a new stance toward life. While this point to the advancement in the way of Leventhal's learning of what it means to be human, his observations on himself also clarify. Bellow's idea on the inescapable complexities of individual existence in a world of masses:

> Well, the world was a busy place...you couldn't find a place in your feelings for everything, or give at every touch like a swinging door, the same for everyone, with people going in and out as they pleased. On the other hand, if you shut yourself up, not wanting to be bothered, then you were like a bear in a winter hole or like a mirror wrapped in a piece of flannel. And like such a mirror, you were in less danger of being broken, but you didn't flash, either. But you had to flash. That was the peculiar thing. Everybody wanted to be what he was to the limit. (p. 85)

Leventhal is learning that 'to be human' means to participate meaningfully with other human beings because it is meaningful participation that a human being can attain true dignity of his self. Leventhal's alienation is thus coming to an end and he is moving toward accommodation.

Through the above affirmative ideas of Leventhal, Bellow further clarifies his idea of what it means to be truly human. Nothing short of meaningful participation can accord a human life its due dignity. Only then one can attain a true state of selfhood. To render order and meaning to one's life one must share responsibility with other human beings. The embarrassing point however is that one must also be prepared while accepting limits of one's own being, to accept blame even for something done unintentional or for something accidental. The acceptance of blame or sharing responsibility only enables one to have a relationship with fellow human beings.

This effect denotes what it means to be human, while implying understanding with and sympathy for one's fellows. This is brotherhood based on love. Bellow's point is that only by such sharing can one attain one's true human stature and a man then earns his dignity. This point is further crystallized in Chapter Ten in which Schlossberg comes to posit some of the important ideas on human nature. One need not take much trouble to discover that most of the ideas thus expressed are those of the novelist himself.

Chapter Ten is crucial for it and finally helps Leventhal to ease his mind and free himself from a state of victimization. A modern man, Leventhal, is a victim, whose severe limitation among others is his inability to know himself. To be human again one must realize one's potentialities as well as limitations. A theatre critic, Schlossberg tries to educate Leventhal through theatre imagery:

> It is bad to be less than human and it's bad to be more than human...good acting is what is exactly human. And if you say I am a tough critic, you mean I have a high opinion of what is human. This is my whole idea. More than human, can you have any use for life? Less than human, you don't either. (pp. 112-13)

The wisdom of Schlossberg is that human life has dignity. It is greatness and beauty too, but on condition that it is human life; neither sub-human nor super human. As usual, Bellow is ambiguous, when he makes Schlossberg say, that, 'Good acting is what exactly human'. The utterance admits several interpretations. One can however say with conviction that what Bellow means by 'good acting' is the playing one's role in exact terms. To put the matter in different way, one should act within imposed limitations and when one acts within limitations, one is expected to act as a human being, not more not less.

Bellow earlier attacked the attempt 'to be more than human' in *Dangling Man* where Joseph first tried to behave as god—more than human—in his ideal constructions and thus removing him from humanity and for that matter, from mortality. In such a state, human life cannot attain dignity. Schlossberg makes the point clear that human life is not 'lousy and cheap', but is greatness and beauty. "Have dignity, you understand me? Choose dignity. No body knows enough to turn it down" (p. 113), Schlossberg remarks. Through him, Bellow thus voices his own conviction and insists upon viewing man's life as 'lousy and cheap'. Not intending to work out a final resolution, what Bellow intends is to reveal the exact human life at present, the novelist in this chapter under consideration manifests an attitude to life, which is positive in implications. It is further emphasized through the reflections of Leventhal on Schlossberg's utterances. Finally, he comes to agree with the journalists' view that 'human meant accountable in spite of many weaknesses'.

Leventhal moves closer to consciousness of which he was earlier short. He now knows not only the meaning of responsibility and truly human, but also the inherent limitations of human being. If one has to suffer, one has to suffer as a human being. Going by the same logic, if one is to assert his identity, he is to assert it as a human being, neither as more than human nor as less than human. Goodness is achieved in the company of other men. And when one does embrace human company one must also share the sense of mutual responsibility. This in turn implies acceptance of limitations as a human being. These limitations make the power of choice for a man a limited one:

> We don't choose to be born...and unless we commit suicide, we don't choose the time to die, either. But having a few choices in between makes you seem less of an accident to yourself. It makes you feel your life is necessary. (p. 159)

Acceptance of limitations only can lead to the rediscovery of self possible. "Know thyself. Everybody knows but no body admits. That's the things". This point is further clarified by Schlossberg:

> Here I'm sitting here and my mind can go around the world. Is there any limit to what I can think? But in another minute I can be dead on this spot. There's a limit to me. But I have to be myself in full. Which is somebody, who dies, isn't it? That's what I was from the beginning. I'm not three people, four people. I was born once and I will die once you want to be two people? More than human? May be it's because you don't know how to be one. (pp. 207-08)

What Schlossberg comes to hint at is the despite the immense inherent possibilities in him, man must accept his sub-angelic position. Man's potentialities can be realized only when he behaves as exactly human. Wanting to assert individuality in a way, that is either more than or less than human, would invite undesired suffering. Such striving is bound to end in futility, Bellow seems to hint. But to attain true human stature, one must be in consciousness because consciousness is life. Not in isolation, but in participation with fellow human beings one can discover his true identity as a human being. It is evident from the above that in his novel, Bellow manifests the sub-angelic in Asa Leventhal less through a conscious awareness of his potentialities by the protagonist himself, but more through the novelist's depiction of him with a power to complete his life in meaningful terms.

Viewed from this angle, despite the gloomy tone of the novel, it is affirmative. Bellow seems to show that a man has to face hurdles and suffer in the way of becoming 'exactly human', and thereby achieving dignity. If man's limitations, like Leventhal's are inherent, so also his potentialities, but he has also within him deep and sincere feelings of responsibility and accountability. His sympathy for his fellow men accords him the dignity of development and the possibility of change.

Although Leventhal still wonders 'who runs things', there is hint that Leventhal has earned the ability to come to terms with whoever runs things. Notwithstanding the seemingly unresolved ending of the novel, Leventhal's union with his pregnant wife is a clear sign of this end. Mary's pregnancy gives promises of new life. There is assurance that Leventhal will be aware of his status in life. The last scene depicting an usher showing Leventhal and his wife the proper way to their seats in theatre hall makes it explicit that Leventhal will now be able to treat the way of life in right direction. Bellow thus carefully charts Leventhal's coming to terms with reality which seems to be the other name of a complex, hostile and disturbing world. Leventhal's sense of isolation has come to an end. One is inclined to hope that Leventhal now will not have the feeling of being 'persecuted'.

Beginning as a solitary, away from his wife and not congenial to friends he has, his transformation can view as an extrasocial one, insofar as his learning to behave exactly human by accepting limitations and sharing responsibility with other human beings, are concerned. He has learned to humble down and has qualified himself for the true human dignity. Bellow in the novel, thus comes up with the message that victimization, whether deliberate or intentional, is a fact of life which each man must acknowledge as a fact. Leventhal thus in a sense, has joined humanity without surrendering to society. Leventhal can discover his identity only when he comes to terms with the world and discovering it, he must relinquish it to the common humanity.

In *The Victim* Bellow shifts the focus of his concern with the problem of the self by deviating from the question of freedom to that of responsibility. The issue of Jewish identity is a collary to this theme. The problem of responsibility deals with the question: Who victimizes whom? and what is the nature of complicity? The issue of accountability is closely linked with the need for the positive values of human dignity, greatness and beauty. In *The Victim* Bellow explores the problem of complicity and human dignity through an intricate pattern of human relationships. The main dramatic context through which the theme of complicity is unfolded is the relationship of Asa Leventhal, the hero with Kirby Allbee, a forgotten acquaintance of the former who blames him for the loss of his job and all the resultant hardships. The issues of responsibility and Jewish identity are interwoven in the novel through the mutually hostile but inescapable bonds which tie Asa and Allbee together. Inextricably interwoven with this plot, is the other strand involving, Asa with the family of his brother, Max. Asa is called upon to take care of his absent brother's family and assume the responsibility for the treatment of his nephew, Mickey who is seriously ill. Even this personal and familial involvement is so deeply ingrained in Asa's Jewishness that one cannot help describing *The Victim* as Bellow's most Jewish novel. However, due to Bellow's concern with the general human predicament and the issues of self in relation to the demands of society on it, the theme of responsibility is treated as much in terms of man-to-man relationship as in terms of an entanglement between a Jew and a Gentile. Even as Allbee, Max and his wife Elena, Elena's mother, and the images of Asa's mother and father serve only to illumine the negative aspect of Jewishness in the novel, the figure of venerable old Jew Schlossberg is a pointer towards the positive values of human dignity, greatness and beauty. In Schlossberg's character Bellow provides guidelines for a standard of conduct which will enable the individual to achieve balance and harmony, although to Asa's inherent inadequacy the novel fails to offer a conclusive or positive solution to the problem of responsibility.

After a lengthy period during which Asa and Allbee have not seen each other, a down-at-the heels Allbee one day appears to hold Leventhal responsible for his downfall. He attributes the loss of his job to an argument between Leventhal and his former employer, Rudiger. Leventhal responds at first with complete denial of responsibility to the matter, attributing Allbee's difficulties to excessive drinking rather than to the disagreement between himself and Rudiger. Soon, however, Leventhal begins to fluctuate between anger and pity especially when he learns that Allbee's wife left him and later died. Leventhal does not acknowledge Allbee's charges. But this denial does not amount to assertiveness on the part of Asa, for he has been always shaky inwardly. He has never had confidence in himself. It is his moderate success that has separated him from others. He is suspicious of others and feels threatened by the fear that he might fall into the condition of the wretched and downtrodden. Although Asa perceives the mental connection with Allbee and is moved a little by the persuasive accusations of Allbee resulting in Asa's self-examination, he has not the strength to withstand the demands of an inner trial nor does he have the clear sightedness to study the issue in all its implications. Harkavy's wisdom only hurts him. His intention to pursue the matter with Williston only subjects him to more fear of being guilty. His thoughts are filled with fears that the verdict of Williston may go against him because he is a Jew which means:

> ...the turn he always feared had come and all good-luck was cancelled and all favours melted away. (p. 79)

Asa's shortsightedness is also due to his ego. Although he tells himself that the inequalities in this world are due to 'a wrong', his ego explains it away as a 'general wrong'.

At a particular stage he becomes sober and tries to understand his own rule in Allbee's matter:

> He recognized one of those deeper issues which he had failed to reach before. He was ready to accept the blame for losing his head at Dill's. But why had lost it? (p. 102)

The correct answer to this question means the beginning of Asa's genuine moral progression and his understanding of the deeper issues of life. It has to mean Asa's freedom from his own ego, from fear, Jewish and psychological, his isolation and guilt, and more significantly, his comprehension of himself through suffering that should lead to love, Asa then will be in a position to accept suffering with human dignity.

But his withdrawal into the past in terms of his personal relationship with his mother and father and his Jewish attitude towards his brother's marriage with a Catholic woman and his suspicion towards his brother's mother-in-law are the confines which further imprison him in his narrow outlook and suffering. Asa also does not spare his brother for his absence and gets harsher towards him from time to time. In the absence of Allbee, he is obsessed with thoughts about his brother's mother-in-law. He clashes mentally with this anti-Jewish entity and suffers from a self-created pain. He even tells his brother to get rid of the woman. He dislikes his father's down to earth attitude of personal gain. Still, like his father, he also feels insecure in a hostile world and makes imaginary enemies. He is held by the pull of a past which he can neither accept nor abandon, nor understand. In fact, *The Victim* can be said to be a study of the haunting influence of the past, for Asa's suffering is due to the accusation of Allbee that the former caused his dismissal deliberately to retaliate the latter's anti-Semitic remarks. For Asa, the past comes to mean a dark world to flee from. As stated by Irving Malin, it is "the 'original sin' which he cannot understand or accept".[2]

As opposed to these constricting influences, the Jewish authority figure of Schlossberg is a pointer towards the positive values of human dignity, greatness and beauty. As stated by Ihab Hassan. "...the most affirmative note in the novel is sounded by minor character, old Schlossberg".[3] Schlossberg checkmates Asa's pride and his inability to establish relationship with others. Leventhal meets this old Jewish journalist in a cafeteria. Schlossberg is concerned with what it is to be exactly human. According to him, one who is divorced from common human sentiments is not human. Good acting means an earnest participation in the plight of others and a response to the sadness and misery of human life. One who is more than human, or less than human, is an alienated man. Julius Caesar rejected human weakness by projecting it onto others, just as Asa did. Asa knows the example of Caesar, but does not realize how he is himself like Caesar in this respect. He does not consciously aim at human greatness through "ideal construction" like Joseph of *Dangling Man*. But in his false pride and refusal to admit that one is like other, he is like Joseph. As Clayton observes:

> Schlossberg's attack on the "more than human" was seen earlier in Bellow's assault on greatness and ideal constructions in *Dangling Man*: man tries to make himself into a god dehumanizing himself to remove

himself from humanity and hence mortality. It is a perfect description of the roots of Joseph's alienation.[4]

Schlossberg says: "More than human, can you have any use for life? less than human, you don't either" (p. 113). He tells Asa not to be "measly", and advises him to have dignity. He says "...have dignity, you understand me? choose dignity" (p. 118), this admission alone that one is not too good for this world leads one to the state of being human.

In *The Victim* this problem of acceptance of the middle state of being human is explored by Bellow through an intricate pattern of human relationships. The two plots serve each other in this regard, as much as they lend a special kind of density to the structure of the novel. Mickey's death is the main bolt holding the two plots together. It is through this incident that a 'showdown' comes for Asa's conscience. The theme of Asa's responsibility for Allbee's loss of job is reinforced by Asa's fears on the possibilities of Mickey's death and the consequent guilt when his fears become true. The responses and feelings caused in Asa by the two situations are so identical that it is difficult to distinguish the one situation from the other Asa keeps telling himself:

> The showdown is coming—guiltily, for at heart he had no hope. The word itself was an evasion, and he, not the doctor, had introduced it. But it was a comprehensive word; it embraced more than Mickey's crisis, or Elena's, or his own trouble with Allbee. They were included; what had been going on with Allbee, for example, could not be allowed to continue indefinitely. But what he meant by this preoccupying 'showdown' was a crisis which would bring an end of his resistance to something he had no right to resist. Illness, madness, and death were forcing him to confront his fault. He had used every means, and principally indifference and neglect, to avoid acknowledging it and he still did not know what it was. (pp. 130-31)

Since "indifference and neglect" are Asa's principal means of resisting "something he had no right to resist", his real guilt is due to his rejection of his responsibility. He participates in the crisis of illness of his nephew with a superiority complex and a condescending attitude to his brother, apart from viewing Elena and her mother with suspicion and fear.

But, with the death of Mickey a transformation takes place in Asa. He comes closer to an understanding of the "human", to an admission that one is not too good for this world. Complementarily, it means responsiveness to the suffering of others. Mickey's death causes for Asa a situation of encounter with the fact of the impermanence of human life. After Mickey's funeral he goes to the park. There he recognizes something human in the open nature and in the music produced by the "band of revivalists".

> There was an overwhelming human closeness and thickness, and Leventhal was penetrated by a sense not merely of the crowd in the part but of innumerable millions crossing, touching, pressing. What was the story he had once read about Hell cracking open on account of the rage of the god of the sea, and all the souls, crammed together, looking out? But these were alive, this young couple with bare arms, this woman late in pregnancy, sauntering, this boot black hauling his box by the long scrap. (p. 151)

The isolated self of Asa has now begun to open towards the multitude. The presence of millions of men felt by Asa has a close analogy with the meaning of the second epigraph of the book which is taken from De Quincey's *The Pains of Opium*:

> ...the sea appeared paved with innumerable faces, upturned to the heavens; faces, imploring, wrathful, despairing faces that surged upward by thousands, by myriads, by generations....

But, ironically, these clearly discernible meanings of Asa's moments of relief remain only in isolation and their meanings become far-fetched due to Asa's basic inability to respond to experience with a sense of objective purpose: hence the absence of any permanent change in Asa's outlook towards either Max or Elena's mother, or Allbee. These moments come like a short-circuit in the mental equipment of Asa which is charged with the negative powers of fear and suspicion. From the park

Asa returns to his apartment and sees the dining room open and "Allbee undressing". His "fear" and "indignation", though short-lived, are replaced by "a state of indifference akin to numbness, and he lay down more conscious of the heat than that of any emotion in himself" (p. 152). He continues to fear Elena's look. He imagines horror on Elena's last look in the Chapel: "People crying when their faces were twisted might appear to be laughing and so on" (p. 155). He feels determined to tell Max to throw out the old woman: "For Philip's sake, Max ought to show the old devil the door" (p. 155). Thus, Asa still continues to live in a world of fears and hatred amounting to nightmares.

In his final meeting with Max, which comes much later, he maintains the same impressions about Elena and the same fears about her mother. Apart from insisting that the old woman should be abandoned, he blames the nurses for not extending adequate care to Mickey. He says, "Those fools.... Not to have somebody posted there" (p. 197). But, "Max excused them with a downward wave of the hand: 'All the nurses didn't know. It's a big place'" (p. 197). Asa is moved by his "half burned" brother and says, "There have been times when I felt life that, too,... That's a feeling that comes and goes" (p. 197). Asa is visibly moved by Max's admission, "...we must have made mistakes, too. But what can we do?" (p. 197) The limitations of man in controlling death are voiced through Max's spirit of acceptance which is not possessed by Asa Elsewhere, Asa feels puzzled as to why God should choose Mickey alone for death. Still, he has not grown wiser to accept determinism in life and view people, like the nurses, as instruments only through whom fate operates and that they do not, therefore, deserve the blame. So far as his change towards Allbee is concerned, the effect of these happenings does not still go beyond his admission of "his unwillingness and inability to deal with Allbee" (p. 199). In other words, Asa has not been willing to recognize his own ethical involvement in Allbee's condition. He has not been able to deal with Allbee due to his absorption in a personal evaluation resulting in self-justifying attitude.

Asa's recognition of his ethical involvement in Allbee's condition has to emerge through a conscious and consistent change in him in order that he may come to feel towards Allbee the same warmth and humility which he feels for Max. It would also amount to Asa's attainment of Schlossberg's standard of human dignity, which is the result of one's acceptance of one's accountability.

During the period of Asa's conflict with Allbee, his consciousness, of course, is exposed to new perspectives of life. His unwillingness to see suffering and evil yielded place to acknowledge of suffering that came through his confrontation with certain aspects of the irrational, the most important of which is Mickey's death. The effort to be more than human amounts to an effort to avoid death. Schlossberg explains:

> There is a limit to me.... I was born once and I will die once. You want to be two people? More than human? May be it's because you don't know how to be one. (p. 208)

Rejection of death turns the reality of life into unreal and makes illusion count for reality just as the "paper grass in the grave makes all the grass paper" (p. 208). Asa does not reconcile himself to the death of Mickey, though it opens his mind towards the "showdown". The old Jewish belief referred to by Allbee that a man suffers for his own faults and that God "is the department of weights and measures" (p. 122) is not useful to Asa, for it does not explain to him the metaphysical absurdity of Mickey's death and the social absurdity of his being held responsible for Allbee's faults. Harkavy also attempts to awaken Asa's consciousness in the name of Jesus Christ and God. He says,

> What's life? Consciousness, that's what it is. That's what you're short on. For God's sake, give yourself a push and a shake. It's dangerous stuff, Asa, this stuff. (p. 214)

Asa's slumber, dullness and innocence constitute the really "dangerous stuff", which is given a jolt from time to time by his conflicts with the irrational. Allbee's sexual act in Asa's room and his attempted suicide are also the facts which bring

Asa face to face which the irrational, providing him with an opportunity to accept that "evil is as real as sunshine" (p. 123), as observed by Allbee himself. It is true that Asa is free from the narrow perspectives that once filled him with a sense of being a victim. But Asa's conduct with Allbee in the final scene does not speak for a total transformation in Asa. He has not transcended his fragmentary outlook towards life. Bellow's presentation of the world as absurd is subjected and restricted to Asa's narrow and fragmentary vision. *The Victim* presents different conflicting points of view through the juxtaposed perspectives of Asa and Allbee.

Asa, of course, has been able to live happily during the preceding years. This happiness may also be attributed to his reunion with Mary whom he longs for throughout the novel, confessing that in her absence he is lost. He tells Max, "I guess, I really don't know where I'm at when she's away" (p. 226). After Allbee leaves him, he becomes much more inpatient for Mary. As he tries to sleep, "his impatience made him groan" (p. 227). He sees the station platform and makes out "Mary's face in the crowd of passengers...he embraced and kissed her... he struggled over a choice of greetings" (p. 227). Asa, like Allbee, is a simple man of several natural deeds. He feels for Mary so deeply and continuously that one may even dismiss the possibility of all the suffering he is made to face due to Allbee. The troubles that had started in Mary's absence all disappeared with his reunion with Mary and this coincides with his disentanglement from Allbee.

The responses of Asa towards Allbee at the end of the novel are rather ambivalent. They are suggestive of his unwillingness to feel hearty about meeting Allbee after a long time. Norman Podhoretz observes that Asa "has not ventured into the 'deaths' that he once feared would drown him: he has merely (like a successfully analyzed patient) learned something about himself that has helped him come to terms with the world and make a settlement".[5] Clayton suggests:

> It is more accurate to say that because he understands that the depths he fears are within him, he does not have to be destroyed by them.[6]

Allbee himself is one such for of destruction for Asa. By throwing him out, he has rejected the evil symbolically and momentarily, for his behaviour towards Allbee at the end does not fully explain whether Asa himself is confident of his ability to coexist and resist the "cannibalistic things" that he thinks of during his life with Allbee.

Towards the end of the novel Asa broods over the empty promises of life. He thinks that tickets are not important, and that

> There were more important things to be promised. Possibly there was a promise, since so many felt it. He himself was almost ready to affirm that there was. But it was misunderstood. (p. 231)

The promise remains undefined, though, Asa momentarily feels the readiness "to affirm that there was" one. One cannot expect Asa to define or discover values through his own spiritual conflicts, for, the growth, which he has achieved, is not felt or understood by Asa himself. Even when Allbee, in the final meeting, profusely and touchingly apologizes and "took Leventhal's hand and pressed it.... Leventhal pulled his hand away" (p. 237). Asa's reluctance here to accommodate certain things in his heart suggests that his troubles are not yet over. He is now able to look at things and listen to men. But he is not free from caution against the cannibalistic things which made really good things unsafe, like those he once saw in Allbee. Asa cannot be expected to shed this caution 'in toto', for *The Victim*, while it is a call to such a vision, does not offer one in men like Asa. Asa is not capable of knowing his seat; he has to be led by somebody to his seat. Allbee runs in towards the stairs, but Asa does not move from where he is.

> The bell continued its dinning, and Leventhal and Mary were still in the aisle when the house lights went off. An usher showed them to their seats. (p. 238)

This subtle image, which concludes the novel, also speaks for the ambivalences which a serious novelist like Bellow probably cannot be expected to resolve through strained arguments or heavy symbolism. It offers a variety of meaning like the need to accept things, whoever runs them, and be conducted by the usher when one gets stranded in darkness. It does not suggest anything concrete in terms of an affirmation of life. Galloway, however, sees a more meaningful conclusion in the undefined "promise". He states that it "...brings *The Victim* to a conclusion more significantly, if as vaguely, affirmative as that of *Dangling Man*."[7] If Asa's fragmentary vision was ultimately yielded the undefined promise and, therefore, has ended the novel more significantly, it still does not clarify the mode of Asa's relationship with the world of which Allbee is the concretized form. Any more expectation on our part may not be justifiable in the given framework of Asa's potentialities. Asa, free from the day-to-day torments of life, provides the reader with a certain sense of relief. If Asa has not realized the significant fruit of his suffering, it is due to his own, in ability to understand. Alfred Kazin realistically sums up the achievement of Asa by stating that

> Asa Leventhal at the end of *The Victim*, having been persecuted, exploited, terrified by a Gentile who accuses the Jew of having persecuted him, ends up innocently saying to his tormentor—"wait a minute, what's your idea of who runs things".[8]

References

1. Saul Bellow, *The Victim* (Harmondsworth, 1984), Subsequent references in parentheses are to this edition.
2. Irving Malin, *Jews and Americans* (Illinois, 1985), p. 73.
3. Ihab Hassan, *Radical Innocence: Studies in the Contemporary American Novel* (Princeton, New Jersey, 1971), p. 302.
4. J.J. Clayton, *Saul Bellow: In Defence of Man* (Bloomington, 1968), p. 146.
5. Norman Podhoretz, *Doings and Undoings: The Fifties and After in American Writing* (New York, 1964), p. 214.
6. J.J. Clayton, *Saul Bellow: In Defence of Man* (Bloomington, 1968), p. 162.
7. David D. Galloway, "The Absurd Man as Picaro", *The Absurd Hero in American Fiction* (Austin, 1970), pp. 93-94.
8. Alfred Kazin, *Bright Book of Life* (New Delhi, 1973), p. 136.

4

The Adventures of Augie March

The Adventures of Augie March (1953), narrated by its title character, chronicles Augie March's adaption to protean changes of circumstances from his childhood in Chicago before the Depression, through the 1930s and 1940s, to his postwar life in Europe as a young married man and a dealer in black-market goods. The people in his life vie with Augie in narrative interest, however, for Augie is self-proclaimedly adoptable, and a procession of vivid strong-willed persons orchestrate the circumstances of his life in an attempt to shape him to their images. Machiavellis of small street and neighbourhood, Augie terms them in an effort to give a theme to the account of his adventures, and he is more ready to tell about them than about himself. Among the family members, only his elder brother Simon rivals these 'adopters' in importance. Neither the simple minded Mrs. March nor Augie's mentally retarted brother Georgie looms as importantly in the narrative as they, for neither qualifies as a Machiavelli.

The first of these strong-willed adopters is Grandma Lausch—not really Augie's grandmother at all, but an elderly Jewish boarder, born in Odessa. She governs the household autocratically, and she commands dutiful affection from Augie and Simon while she indoctrinates them in an idiosyncratic compound of Horatio Alger idealism and streetwise opportunism when she can no longer hold the family together with the force of her personality, her last mental institution. Then, savouring bitterly her apparent failure to make something of Simon and Augie, she withdraws to a home for the aged and forgets the Marches, although not herself forgotten by Augie.

The second Machiavelli in Augie's life is William Einhorn, under whose influence Augie falls when he takes a job with him in his last years of high school. The Einhorn is crippled in both arms and legs and has to be dressed, carried about, and even taken to the toilet by Augie does not interfere with his management of varied business interests. Nor does Einhorn's disability mitigates his avid search for the woman in the world whom he might turn to a quivering mass of lust. Indeed, he is a man of vivid contradictions. Augie credits him with 'statesmanship, fineness of line, Parsee sense, deep-dug intrigue, and the scorn of Pope Alexander VI for custom.' He notes also a sense of the dollar that inspires Einhorn to install a pay telephone in his office for the use of visiting businessman.

Einhorn's influence over Augie is never entirely broken, but after Augie graduates from high school, his influence is temporarily superseded by that of Mr. and Mrs. Renling, who employ Augie as a salesman in their fashionable saddleshop. Mrs. Renling in particular adopts Augie, and under her tutelage he learns to dress, talk, and move in manner to which he was not born. He is even taken by Mrs. Renling to exclusive Benton Harbor in the ostensible role of companion, so determined are the Renlings to make Augie their own, that they finally offer to adopt him legally, but at that point Augie flees.

After leaving the Renlings, Augie works briefly as a paint salesman and then falls in with an inept gangster named Joe Gorman and a scheme to assist illegal immigrations from Canada. Drifling back to Chicago after a brush with the Detriot police, he moves into a student boarding house on the south side, resumed attending university classes, and support himself by petty theft from bookstores, a skill in which he is trained by a friend named Padilla. The main adopter in this phase of his life is his brother Siman, who marries into the wealthy Magnus family and persuades Augie to work for him in the coal yard he is given by the Magnuses as a dowry. Simon picks out Augie's clothe with a paternalism reminiscent of Mrs. Renling's, and he even engages Augie romantically with another Magnus daughter in an effort to strengthen ties to the family.

Augie eliminates a chance he never really wanted to marry into the Magnus family when he helps a fellow boarder named Mimi Villars to find an abortionist and is generally assumed to be the father of her unborn child. Fired by Simon for the disrepute this brings him with the Magnuses, he works briefly as a housing surveyor for the WPA, then as labour organizer for the CIO. He also becomes involved with Thea Fenchel, an apparently wealthy Jewish girl he had first met at Benton Harbor and who had recently established herself in a Chicago hotel in order to renew acquaintance with Augie while awaiting a Mexican divorce decree. She is clearly another adopter, but when goons from the rival AFL attack Augie at a union meeting, he runs to Thea and allows himself to be drawn into her madcap plan for learning to hunt with an eagle in Mexico. Against all advice, newly aware that Thea's money is all her husband's but fancying himself in love, Augie joins her expedition.

Although Thea is a devoted and able trainer, an eagle they purchase and name Caligula proves a coward, and the Mexican adventure gradually palls. Secretly hating the whole business and openly in revolt when Thea disowns Caligula and begins to collect poisonous snakes, Augie begins in Chilpanzingo to go his own way. When he helps an acquaintance named Stella Chesney in potential difficulty with Mexican authorities to escape the country, Thea suspects rightly that he and Stella have been lovers and leaves him. To be abandoned rather than adopted is a disorienting experience for Augie, and in the wake of Thea's departure he is briefly unhinged from reality.

Events move more quickly in the last five chapters of the novel. Returning to Chicago from Mexico, Augie finds Simon eager to take charge once again of his younger brother's life. Evading such a take over, Augie accepts a job as research assistant with an eccentric millionaire named Robey and helps him to research a projected history of human happiness. Sophie Geralis, an old friend from his days as a labour organizer, wants to marry Augie, and clean Tambow, another old friend, wants him to collaborate in a vocational-guidance scheme, but Augie is shrewder now than before about his adoptability and sidesteps their plans. With the advent of World War II, he joins the merchant marine. On his first liberty leave, he visits Stella Chesney in New York and falls deeply in love. They are married day after his graduation from training school but have to separate several days later when Augie ships out of Boston.

When Augie's ship is torpedoed and sunk on the fifteenth day out of Boston, he shares a lifeboat with a mad scientist named Basteshaw, who proves to be still another adopter. Basteshaw wants to sail for the Canary Islands and be incarcerated for the war so that he can continue his lunatic research into the creation of life, and he decides that Augie will be research assistant. When Augie expresses a preference for rescue, Basteshaw overcomes him and lies him up, Augie eventually frees himself and is picked up by a British tanker. The last chapter of the novel finds him living happily in Europe with Stella and working for a blackmarketeer, Mintouchian.

In *The Adventures of Augie March* Bellow shifts to an open form in contrast to the closed ones in his two earlier novels. This is in consonance with the overall mental make up of the present protagonist for search of identity and self knowledge makes him a free wheeler in life. Augie March tries to find out who and what he is and thereby discover the true stature of his self. The journey of the hero is towards self knowledge which may finally lead to a fuller realization of his love for life and joy of living. From this viewpoint, the novel celebrates joy, hope and freedom. Chapter Four has thrown much light on the aspect that Augie's ethnic past has given his American character a unique stamp. The city bred American Jew, while en route on the discovery of his self, declares that a man's character is his fate:

> I am an American, Chicago born—Chicago that somber city—and go at things as I have taught myself, free style,

> first to knock, first admitted.... But a man's character is his fate. (*AAM*, p. 3)

With this aphorism, Augie starts his adventures. But notwithstanding, the jubilant tone of the novel, like Bellow's earlier heroes who choose to play the role of the looser, Augie too cannot accept success and rejects position of status. He rather chooses to maintain the primal innocence of his heart and makes an honest attempt to maintain the integrity of his self, rather than falling prey to other's scheme. One is inclined to believe that such a temperament is an inborn one not only with Augie but with most of Bellow's heroes. Even in his teens, he disappointed Anna Coblin who wanted to adopt him as her son-in-law. His search for identity had already taken a firmer root in him. This he calls a good enough fate:

> Even at that time I couldn't imagine that I would marry into the Coblin family. And when Anna snatched Howard's saxophone, my thought was, go on, take it. What do I want it for. I'll do better than that my mind was already dwelling on a good enough fate. (p. 28)

Augie's search for identity thus takes the shape of 'a good enough fate' after which, he strives. When one observes that Augie's striving comes into conflict with the people around him, one can view thus as an average man's attempt at social adjustment. In other words, through the adventures of Augie, Bellow examines the issue of socio-individual adjustment in the present environment. To be sure, asserting one's individuality in the face of crowd in a mass-society has become hard task indeed. People like Augie are however committed to this task with sincerity.

Augie remains true to the task of the discovery of the self. It makes him perform several roles in his life. His experiences are thus many and varied. Augie helps to rob a store and associates himself with gangsters. He then earns his bread at the University of Chicago by stealing books. He becomes a demonstrator for sometime and again he is chauffeur to a dog's club. He becomes a union organizer in a Chicago hotel and later secretary-cum-writer to an eccentric millionaire. But much before he was drawn to such a vast sphere of roles, he had to face the theoreticians whom he would prefer to call the Machiavellians. Six or seven characters in the novel appear before him as reality instructors and try to educate him in the way of the world.

Among the characters who belong to above category, there are Grandma Lausch, his brother Simon and Anna Coblin from his family side. Again there are Einhorn, the Renlings, Thea and Mimi Villars who take upon themselves the task of educating him. His reaction to and rejection of the schemes of Grandma Lausch and Simon have already been amplified in Chapter Four. While Grandma dies leaving her project of educating Augie incomplete, it is his love for his brother, that Augie moves along with him for a while but he cannot commit himself to his brother's schemes because he has no fundamental belief in such business schemes. That his relation with Mimi Villars remains, by and large, at a friendly level and that his relationship with Thea became a failure, have also been shown in the preceding chapter. Especially to Thea he appeared to be no special one as he rejected her plans for him and declined to be filled into her schemes. Nevertheless, Augie's fate brings him into contact with all of these people. All of these people appear to be adoptive toward Augie. Augie realizes it before hand and remarks ironically:

> All the influences were lived up waiting for me. I was born and there were to form me.... (p. 43)

Bellow's point in the novel is to focus on the struggle of Augie against such world influences in order to maintain the integrity of his self.

After Grandma Lausch Einhorn is the first superior man who tries to instruct him and mould his life. Like Grandma, he takes upon himself the role of educating Augie:

> Einhorn had a teaching turn similar to Grandma Lausch, both believing they could show what could be done with the world, where it gave or resisted where you could be confident and run or where you could only feel your way and forced to blunder. (p. 67)

Einhorn is a semi-corrupt entrepreneur who believes in the power of America free enterprise. He compares the businessman to “the conqueror, the poet and philosopher and assumes that business offers a world of possibilities” (p. 67). Augie has to spend sometime with Einhorn as his all purpose secretary and at first begins to flourish under his influence. Einhorn preaches him optimistically about “the machine age and the kind of advantage that had to be taken of it and Augie seems to receive gladly the preaching from the learned signor” (p. 72). But Einhorn's optimism is shattered by the loss in his business and he is compelled to cut out Augie who is now a luxury for him. Before leaving Einhorn however, the latter reveals a truth about Augie that he has the impulse to say ‘no’:

> This was the first time that any one had told me anything like the truth about myself, I felt it powerfully that as he said, I did have opposition in me and great desire to offer resistance and to say ‘No’. (p. 117)

Although he feels a sort of love for the discovery of this truth in him, he cannot agree with the version of reality that Einhorn comes to preach him. Especially after his fall in business, Einhorn appears to be more sinister even than Grandma. Augie states about Einhorn who now:

> ...intended that as there were no more effective prescriptions in old ways as we were in dreamed out of finished visions, that therefore, in the naked form of human jelly, one should choose or seize with force from disadvantages and make progress by having enemies being wrathful or terrible. (p. 183)

It is unthinkable for Augie to adopt such an attitude toward life. More than this he rejects Einhorn's idea on him that he prefers determination:

> No I didn't want to be what he called determined. I never had accepted determination and wouldn't become what other people wanted to make of me. I had said ‘No’ to Joe Gorman too. To Grandma. To Jimmi. To lots of people Einhorn had seen this in me because he too wanted to exert influence. (pp. 117-18)

Augie leaves Einhorn to have his next encounter with the Renlings. Mrs. Renling comes up with a keen desire of making Augie a refined gentleman. Like Grandma, she wants to offer him education and culture. Even more she wants to make Augie 'completely perfect'. However, Augie soon discovers that Mrs. Renling too was 'adoption minded' and when she directly proposes adoptions, he is reluctant to bow down:

> Just when Mrs. Renling's construction around me was nearly complete, I shoved off. The leading and precipitating reason was that she proposed to adopt me. I was supposed to become Augie Renling live with them, and inherit all their dough. (p. 115)

Naturally, Augie rejects such prospect of success, as it cannot fit into his idea of a fate good enough:

> I was in state of removal from all her intentions for me. Why should I turn into one of these people who didn't know who themselves were? And the unvarnished truth is that it wasn't a fate good enough for me. (p. 151)

While rejecting Mrs. Renling's idea of adoption, Augie makes some general observations. These are high significant in so far as these reveal the radical tension between the individual and society. One of Bellow's preoccupations in his novels:

> I was not going to build into Mrs. Renling's world to consolidate what she affirmed she was. And it is not only she but a class of people who trust they will be justified, that their thoughts will be as substantial as the seven hills to build on, and by spreading their power, they will have an eternal city.... (pp. 151-52)

Augie's rich inner vision forbids him to fall a prey to such false temptations. Mrs. Renling, like Grandma Lausch, therefore, thinks of Augie as a fool.

Here one can offer the view that the ideas expressed by Grandma and Mrs. Renling are not in consonance with Augie's standard of heart. Augie's rejection of other's scheme cannot be said to be an act of glory. Far from it, it denotes the expression of a basic human innocence which Augie carries deep within his heart. It is the integrity of the self that Augie values most. By juxtaposing the basic human honesty through his protagonists with the harsher reality, Bellow wants to vindicate that values still matter. Innocence may meet with failure on the superficial level but it still counts so as to enable one to examine the degree of inherent possibility of the self. Bellow makes Augie stick to his innocence and means to propose that it is only through the primal innocence of heart that a man can attempt at the salvation of his soul.

The inherent opposition in Augie leads him to pass beyond the Machiavellians who seek to enlist him under the laws of control and limitations. He drifts in and out of a number of adventures all of which proffer a fate to him. But none of these fates is good enough for Augie—they all threaten imprisonment by imposed restrictions on his views of life. It is true that the reality instructors fail to share his optimism. Nevertheless, with the growing maturity, he is soon forced to learn that life is brutal and no one can remain as idealistic and innocent as he had been. In course of time, he will be forced by the trauma he suffers to realize this further. Ironically, it is his wish to embrace the quality of texture of life that leads him further to confront the harsher reality.

Leaving the Renlings, he has to face financial hardship. His finer sensibility makes him feel a sense of displacement in a modern city existence, where there is 'more than it be'. He senses a threat to his self and rightly reflects that the main problem of a city bred person is to resist the loss of self, which he feels, can be done in two ways, either the self can be merged into the crowd, or conversely it can retreat into a self-imposed isolation devoid of any sensibility. Augie in such a state does not get money even from Simon and under pressure of existence, he takes to book stealing. But even then he cannot forsake his striving for a separate destiny a higher destiny. Augie still relates the freedom of choice and in a conflict between the ideal and the real, he votes in favour of the former.

Augie therefore fails in book-stealing business because he starts "reading them too". In fact, it is his dedication to a high ideal which lends him strength to say 'no' to a host of people from Grandma to Renlings to Simon. He struggles to uphold those qualities that he considers to be the most human, tenderness and dignity. Just as he rejected Einhorn's ideas to make strength from disadvantages and make progress by having enemies, so also he cannot take Simon's advice to cheat the honest customers. Augie's commitment, if any, is to his own self and to his higher fate. For this, he must remain true to himself. This search for his identity—striving for a fate good enough intimates his quest and is the motive for his rejecting the limited fates offered by the other people. While his idealistic self admits of a bond with the large humanity, he feels reluctant to reconcile himself with society, that offers narrower version of the self. Hence he is a material failure and his quest for a better fate is rendered difficult by the nature of the crippling society he is born into.

What Bellow presents through adventures of Augie is the fact that the individual self is continually pushed, drawn or threatened by other people's version of what life is for and how it should be led. It is a world of materialists where exploitation is the rule for the sake of more money. Not to make material progress is to be a fool. His brother Simon stands at the other pole. Simon makes money by fair or foul means and reveals its corrupting influences in so far as it brutalizes a man and devalues his life. Like in his other novels, Bellow draws on the abstract power of money that he has cut across everywhere—love, family, happiness, self-respect. Augie is thus a failure not only in his personal and emotional life, but in his material life as well. Viewed from this angle, Augie is a rebel hero who would not submit his individuality to the corrupting forces of the world. With all his involvement, he remains true to his search for a separate destiny and keeps himself detached in saying 'no' to everyone who wants to tame him.

Such gestures of Augie can be viewed as taking to rebellion as part of his identity seeking. He demands for him, 'ideal condition' because, he feels nothing restrains people from demanding it, and tries to examine his possibility by being a person who can stand before the terrible appearances:

> You have to plot in your heart to come out differently. External life being so mighty the instruments so huge and terrible, the performances so great, the thoughts so great and threatening. You produce someone who can exist before it. You invent a man who can stand before the terrible appearances. This way he cannot get justice and he can't give justice, but he can live. And this is what mere humanity always does. (pp. 401-02)

Accepting that the structure of human self has become smaller in the face of a huge technological civilization, Bellow once again vindicates his faith in the potentialities of the self. Man still has the possibilities within him and still can afford to exercise this even in the face of a mammoth technological advancement. Augie is too conscious of the protean aspect of existence and himself feels over-powered by things and objects:

> ...in this modern power of luxury with its battalions of workers and engineers, it's the things themselves, the products that are distinguished and the individual man isn't bearly equal to their great sum. Finally they are what becomes great.... No opposing greatness is allowed, and the disturbing person is the one who won't serve by using or denies by not wishing to enjoy. (p. 238)

The last sentence is significant in so far as refers to Augie himself. Despite his awareness of the distracting forces of a modern existence, Augie like his author is life affirming, love affirming and individual affirming. Augie has his human tenderness and he longs for the human. Notwithstanding his constant impulse to say 'no', there is deep with Augie, a feeling to share—of making life disciplined in meaningful participation. Bellow is explicit that even in the face of dehumanized forces of the present civilization the self can attain and retain its true human dignity. However he hints that one cannot have one's self founded on dignity in his 'ideal construction', though at the first instance, a man may be inclined towards such a construction. In such a construction, Bellow implies, a man is isolated from humanity and therefore he ignores his mortality. But to attain dignity for one's self, one must communicate to and participate with other human beings. In other words, he must accept imposed limitations:

> Everyone tries to create a world he can live in and what he can't use he can't see. But the real world is already created, and if your fabrication doesn't correspond, then even if you feel noble and insist on. There being better than what the people call reality, that better something needn't try to exceed what in its actuality, since we know it so little may be very surprising. If a happy state of things, surprising, if miserable or tragic, no worse than what we invent. (p. 318)

True, one has to live a human life as it is not more, not less. It is only by behaving exactly human that one can realize one's potentialities. While depicting the other side of the picture, Bellow comes to hint that society at present seldom promotes such striving. The extent of corruption in the present society hardly attaches any importance to values on which human life must be based. In this connection, Augie's friend Padilla makes a significant revelation which can be applied not only to Augie, but to all of his heroes:

> The big investigation today is into how bad a guy can be, not how good he can be. You don't keep up with the times. You're going against history. Or at least you should admit how bad things are which you don't do either. (p. 431)

The reason why Augie cannot adjust to reality, is revealed by his another friend Clem Tambo. He hints that it is their search for values, that people like Augie cannot cope with the reality as it exists, which no doubt appear to be in its debased form for the seekers like Augie:

> What I guess about you is that you have a nobility syndrome. You can't just adjust to the reality situation. I can see it all over you. You want there should be Man with capital M with great stature. (p. 434)

The meaning of human has shrunk because of the increasing abstractions and specialization of modern life coupled with the technological revolution. Seeking the whole meaning of life, Augie finds only specialized interpretation of it. When Clem Tambo tells that he is not 'concrete enough' and that you're going to ruin yourself ignoring the reality principle, Augie, despite his awareness of the smaller stature of man at present, is affirmative:

> It can never be right to offer to die, and if that's what the data of experience tell you, then you must get along without them. I also understand what you're driving at about my not being concrete. It is as follows: In the world of today your individual man has to be willing to illustrate a more and more narrow and restricted point of existence. And I am not a specialist. (p. 436)

By all his efforts, Augie tries to maintain the integrity of his self. He therefore resists the attempt of other people to tame him. When he talks of the present meagre human existence in the face of the large technical advancements to his one-time neighbour Kayo Obermark, the later unfolds yet another truth before him:

> What you are talking about is Moha a Navajo world, and also Sanskrit, meaning opposite of the finite. It is the Bronx cheer of the conditioning forces. Love is the only answer to Moha, being infinite. I mean all forms of love, Eros, a gape, libido, philia and ecstasy. They are always the same but sometimes one quality dominates and sometimes another. (p. 450)

Augie has meanwhile come to realize that 'the reason for solitude can only be reunion'. The revelation made by Obermark strikes him very much. That Obermark's saying has a lasting effect on him is revealed later when he talks of the axial lines of life:

> I have a feeling...about the axial lines of life with respect to which you must be straight or else your existence is merely clownery, hiding tragedy. I must have had a feeling since I was a kid about these axial lines which made me want to have my existence on them and so I have said 'no' like a stubborn fellow to all my pursuaders...but lately I have felt these thrilling lines again. When striving stops, there they are as gift. I was

> lying on the couch here before and they suddenly went quivering right straight through me. Truth, peace, love, bounty, usefulness harmony, and all noise and grates, distortion, chatter, distraction, effort, superfluity, passed off something like unreal. And I believe that any man at any time can come back to these axial lines, even if an unfortunate bastard, if he will be quiet and wait it out. The ambition of something special and outstanding I have always had is only a boast that distorts this knowledge from its origin.... At any time life can come together again and man, may be regenerated, and doesn't have to be a good or public servant...but the man himself, finite and tape as he is, can still come where the axial lines are. (pp. 454-55)

Conforming to his creator's immense faith in the power of imagination, Augie too falls on his inner resources to suddenly discover some hidden truth that makes his re-discovery of the self-possible. This illumination brings him to acknowledge the sub-angelic position of man. Now he learns to submit and to exert his potentialities within limits. With his humanistic outlook Bellow's hero has learnt to come to terms with life. Affirming his faith in life based on love, Augie has qualified himself to join humanity. He is optimistic about the fate of men in the present century:

> He will be brought into focus. He will live with true joy. Even his plains will be joy if they are true even his helplessness will not take away his power, even wandering will not take him away from himself, even the bog social jokes and hoaxes need not make him ridiculous, even disappointment after disappointment need not take away his love. Death will not be terrible to him if life is not. Thembrace of other true people will take away his dread of fast change and short life. (p. 455)

By these utterances, Augie in fact vindicates his faith in the continuation of human existence against all voids. He seems to hint that the true powerful weapon to fight the void in modern times is love and touch of true human heart. He has learnt this lesson by putting himself into test:

> And this is not the imaginary stuff...because I bring my entire life to the test. (p. 455)

His alienation has come to an end. He has learnt that life becomes meaningful only in participation:

> ...a man could spend forty, fifty, sixty years like that inside walls of his own being. All great experience would only take place within the walls of his being. And all high conversation would take place within those walls. And all glamour too. This would be on it a terrible, hideous dream about existing. (p. 455)

Augie thus makes it explicit that not in isolation but in participation a human life can attain its order and meaning. It is dialogue and not monologue that renders a human self its true dignity. At the same time he makes it clear that although one may require to relinquish part of his identity to participate in dialogue with his fellow beings, it does not necessary mean that by this he loses his dignity:

> All I want is something my own, and bethink myself.... I want a place of my own. I'd take and go to Greenland, and I'd never loan myself again to any other guy's scheme. (p. 456)

With his hope of setting up a home for his family and children, he is still affirmative. Starting his journey in search of a worthwhile fate, he has come to acquire a newer vision. This is indicated by the transposing his declaration "Man's character is his fate" into "Man's fate is his character":

> I said when I started to make the record...that a man's character was his fate. Well then it is obvious that this fate, for what he settles for, is also his character. And since I never have had any place of rest it should follow that I have trouble being still, and further more my hope is based upon getting to be still so that the axial lines can be found. When striving stops, the truth comes as a gift-bounty, harmony, love and so forth. (p. 514)

Augie comes to place his faith in the meaning of human life. He remains as honest at the end of the novel as he was at the beginning. By this, he seems to show that even if people cannot change reality there still remains way of making life meaningful. Even in an age like this, human self is capable of redemption. Augie at the first instance insists on a better fate and vehemently resists temptations of falling prey to other's scheme because his will to oppose is stronger than his will to be a recruit. By rejecting wealth and success, if he acts as a Schlemiel, at the same time he assumes the role of a rebel to assert his individuality, which act implies, in turn, his persistent attempt to uphold individual dignity and values in a corrupting society. Augie's last utterances are significant in that in search of Man with capital M. He compares himself with Colombus, the external voyager, who remained faithful to his own vision even as he was led away in chains:

> Look at me going everywhere. Why, I am a sort of Colombus of those near-at-hand and believe you can come to them in this immediate terra-in-cognita that spreads out in every gaze. I may well be a flop at this line of endeavor. Colombus too thought he was a flop, probably, when they sent him back in chains, which didn't prove there was no America. (p. 536)

Augie thus comes to express his unending faith in the power of inner self, which for him, defines and contains reality. His final claim that he is a sort of Colombus symbolically reflects his indomitable spirit of optimism and also a gesture by which he acknowledges the joke life plays on man and still indicating his refusal to be defeated by it. With clear eyed awareness of the complexity of his situation and therefore a modern man's, he still hopes to continue his search for a meaningful life. If he has not found it yet, it does not mean that it does not exist.

Reference

Bellow, Saul, *The Adventures of Augie March* (Ludhiana, 1953). Subsequent references in parentheses are to this edition.

5

Seize the Day

Seize the Day (1956) chronicles one day in the life of Tommy Wilhelm, a man born into a Jewish family and named Wilhelm Adler at birth. Now in his middle forties and renamed Tommy Wilhelm in a fruitless bid for Hollywood stardom, he is unemployed, financially embarrassed, and separated from his wife Margaret and his two children. He lives temporarily in the hotel Gloriana on Manhattan's West Side, where a vast population of old men and women have established geriatric hegemony. Most notable among the elderly residents of the Gloriana are Dr. Adler, Wilhelm's father, and Dr. Tamkin a dubiously credentialed psychiatrist who dabbles in the stock market.

In the first three chapters, Wilhelm talks at breakfast with his father and is refused both the financial assistance and the emotional support for which he pleads. Dr. Adler is adamant and he will not have his retirement disturbed. His advice to his son is to patronize the Russian and Turkish baths in the Gloriana. He says:

> Simple water has a calming effect and would do you more good than all the barbiturates and alcohol in the world.

Flashbacks striate these chapters illumining Wilhelm's aborted college education, his dealings with a sleazy talent scout named Maurice Venice and his wife's demands upon his non-existent income.

In the next three chapters Wilhelm receives from Dr. Tamkin the emotional and financial assistance denied by his father. On Wilhelm's request, Tamkin has invested his last seven hundred dollars on a joint venture in the stock market and during a second breakfast, a subsequent visit to the brokerage and then lunch, Wilhelm is inundated with Tamkin's advice, both financial and personal. After lunch he discovers that Tamkin's bad advice in the market has wiped him out and that Tamkin has disappeared. In the last chapter, he searches out his father in the Gloriana's steam room, only to have his plea for help rejected summarily. Dr. Adler accuses his son:

> You want to make yourself into my cross. But I am not going to pick up a cross. I'll see you dead, Wilky, by Christ, before I let you do that to me.

In a telephone conversation about a post dated cheque he had sent her, Wilhelm's wife is as unsympathetic as Dr. Adler. Reeling from these rejections, Wilhelm searches the streets for Tamkin and finds himself swept by a crowd into a funeral chapel. The climatically, he begins to weep, 'past words, past reason, past coherence'. But it is a 'happy oblivion of tears' and he sinks in ecstatic abandon 'through torn sobs, and cries towards the consummation of his heart's ultimate need'.

Seize the Day records the case history of failure of its victim hero Tommy Wilhelm. Bellow again moves to closed form to depict the existential crisis of man in a modern city environment. In contrast Augie celebrates freedom and hope, Wilhelm celebrates the weariness, the fever and the fret of contemporary experience. Through his protagonist, Bellow depicts the inner tensions generating from the conflict between natural human demands and the brutal pressures exerted by the world of business, power and money. Man has to fight for his identity in such a world. It is a world where without money; one can hardly attain one's human dignity. Here man is placed face to face with his inescapable condition.

In his middle forties, Tommy Wilhelm is without any position and lives with his retired father Dr. Adler in Hotel Gloriana, where mostly the retired people live. Comparatively young, Wilhelm 'feels out of place' in the hotel. Because his life has been a sequence of mistakes and failures, he has to urge upon his heard hearted father to carry him on. Right from his maiden attempt to build up his career in films at Hollywood, he has witnessed nothing but failures:

> Ten such decisions made up the history of his life. He had decided that it would be a bad mistake to go to Hollywood, and then he went. He had made up his mind not to marry his wife, but ran off and got married. He had resolved not to invest money with Tamkin and then had given him a check (*SD*, p. 27).

His whole life has thus been a series of unsuccessful choices. At this point one can hold that all such actions of Wilhelm manifest his desire for the achievement and recognition of his individuality. His move to make a film career at Hollywood against everyone's advice and even against his own judgement and his change of name from Wilhelm Adler to Tommy Wilhelm a bid for liberty—were nothing but his attempt to fulfill his desire to assert his individuality. But Bellow makes the point that the idea of freedom is limited and also paradoxical. Wilhelm could be successful only partially. While his father would not accept such a change, Wilhelm realizes that man's power is very limited:

> ...there's very little that a man can change at will. He can't change his lungs, or nerves, or constitution, or temperament. They're not under his control. When his young and strong and impulsive and dissatisfied with the way things are he wants to rearrange them to assert his freedom. He can't over throw the government, or be a differently born; he only has a little scope and may be a forebiding too, that essentially can't change. (p. 29)

What Wilhelm discovers finally is that no one can assert his individuality in an absolute manner. Because no one can escape from his inescapable self:

> ...he knew it was his bid for liberty. After being in his mind the title of the species, Tommy the freedom of the person. But Wilky was in his inescapable self. (p. 29)

Like his bid for liberty he has been a failure in other corners of life too. He had never won. Not once.

The powerless son, therefore, has to beg before his powerful but heartless father. His father Dr. Adler epitomizes the power of money in the present day world. The mental gap between the father and the son being already focused, here one can stress the fact that money has been a forceful factor in making Dr. Adler a heartless fellow, Wilhelm feels that the authority he exerts on him has been rendered to him by money. It is money or nothing:

> How they love money, thought Wilhelm. They adore money. Holy money! Beautiful money! It was getting so that people were feeble minded about everything except money. While if you didn't have it you were a dummy, a summy. You had to excuse yourself from the face of earth Chicken! That's what it was. The world's business. If only he could find a way out of it. (p. 41)

Crushed down to the ground by the inhuman pressure of the world's business he looks up to his father with hope for kindness. Dr. Adler, another reality instructor figure in Bellow's novel appears to be devoid of any human heart and instead of helping his son, he comes to list out his son's fault's:

> I can't give you any money. There would be no end to it if I started. You and your sister would take last buck from me. I am still here. Life isn't over yet. I am as much alive as you or anyone. And I want no body on my back. Get off! And I give you the same advice, Wilky carry no body on your back. (p. 61)

In the figure of his father, Wilhelm gets a constant reminder of the demands that the external world makes on a man. Dr. Adler while suggesting the superficialities of urban system has come to symbolize the power of money in a modern city existence. It is an environment where human relationship has come to be measured in terms of money. Here measure of man goes by money standard:

> No, but you hate me. And if I had money you wouldn't. By God, you have to admit it. The money makes the

> difference. Then we would be fine father and son if I was a credit to you—so you could boast and brag about me all over the hotel. But I'm not the right type of son. (p. 61)

The claims of the maternal world have been unbearable for Wilhelm. His much tortured soul longs to be out of this materialistic city life. New York has become a money sucking, crushing and self-centred city. He repeatedly tells his father that it has been unendurable for him to live in New York any more. He feels that he does not belong to New York. What he longs for is a country life based on simplicity, where not money but human warmth rules life:

> New York is like a gas. The colors are running. My head feels so tight. I don't know what I'm doing. He thinks I want to take away his money or that I envy him. He doesn't see what I want. (p. 57)

Bellow here makes one aware of the sheer material pressure and the exhausting physical experience of life in New York. Seeking to live his life on decent terms, the decaying New York would not allow Wilhelm such a possibility. New York appears to him as the end of the world, that must rests on values:

> ...the end of the world with its complexity and machinery, bricks and tubes, wires and stones, holes and heights. And was everybody crazy here? What sort of people did you see? Every other man spoke a different language entirely his own, which he had figured out by his private thinking; he had his own ideas and peculiar ways. (p. 91)

Here only God is mammon and there is no touch of the human heart. The negative forces of city life hinder man from pursuing values and upholding human dignity. Wilhelm finds himself caught in a world devoid of heart, a world where there is no real communication between man and man. Trickery and deception are the only rules here. People talk and do business but all superficially. There is no understanding and no compassion. There is frustration and no love. Human is never reached and Wilhelm finds no way out:

> You had to translate and translate, explain and explain, and it was the punishment of the hell itself not to understand or be understood, not to know the crazy from the sane, the wise from the fools, the young from the old or the sick from the well. The fathers were no fathers and the sons no sons. You had to talk with yourself in the time and reason with yourself at night. Who else was there to talk to in a city like New York. (p. 91)

It is not hard to guess from the above that what Wilhelm wants to continue his life is not money but something else, which the drab city existence cannot provide him. More than money it is love and compassion which can add to the life of Wilhelm. Bellow makes it crystal clear that even on the verge of suffocation, man wants to continue his life as a true human being:

> The spirit, the peculiar burden of his existence lay upon him like an accretion a load, a hump. In any moment of quiet, when sheer fatigue prevented him from struggling, he was apt to feel this mysterious weight, this growth or collection the business of his life to carry about. That must be what a man was for. And man must know the purpose of his life the reason of his existence. Alienated and weighed down by the pressure of the world, Wilhelm too has this sort of quest. (p. 44)

Because he wants to carry on his 'peculiar burden of his existence' and is baffled by the unfeeling behaviour of his father, he falls upon Dr. Tamkin, the Charlatan who leads a shaddy existence as a psychologist and healer and a carrier of idea. Dr. Tamkin becomes his second father who takes upon himself the task of healing Wilhelm. He promises Wilhelm salvation financial and otherwise and thereby brings an end to the anguish of his suffering soul. Tamkin's ideas, therefore, will be healing ideas. And Wilhelm sees a ray of hope in Tamkin, his present 'friend, philosopher and guide'. Alienated from New York city and refused by his father, Wilhelm finds in Dr. Tamkin, a person whom he can talk to. Under persuasion of Dr. Tamkin, Wilhelm buys three orders of land in the commodities market. Tamkin starts his lesson of making Wilhelm alert to enable him to see the present:

> The whole secret of this type of speculation...in the alterness. You have to act fast, buy it and sell it; sell it and buy it again. But quick...strike and strike again. (pp. 72-73)

One has to learn how to act in the present day world of money to catch it. There's money everywhere. Everyone is shoveling it in. After so much bad luck, weariness, weakness and failure at the most nadir of his existence, first uncertain and undecided about relying on Tamkin, Wilhelm gradually comes under the spell of the common Tamkin. He gives Dr. Tamkin a power of attorney over his last seven hundred dollars to speculate for him in the commodities market.

It is Tamkin who in his lecturing process, teaches Wilhelm what reality is. His spiritual father opens up new avenue of awareness in Wilhelm by unfolding what is real in the present day America:

> The real universe. That's the present moment. The past is no good to us. The future is full of anxiety. Only the present is real—the here—and—now. Seize the day. (p. 73)

But Wilhelm is far from being able to seize the present in a dehumanized world. The relentless pursuit of money promotes here the absence of genuine love and any sensitive individual suffers from terrifying isolation from his fellowmen. Tamkin observes:

> ...the lonely person begins to feel like animal. When the night comes...he feels like howling from his window like a wolf. (p. 73)

Tamkin's mission is to provide insights into the inner working of the soul and its relation to its social surroundings. Wilhelm is captivated by what Tamkin reveals about the human soul:

> In the human bosom...there's just one soul. There's a lot of souls. But there are two main ones, the real soul and pretender soul. (p. 77)

Tamkin further teaches Wilhelm:

> Everyman realizes that he has to love something or somebody. He feels that he must go outward. If thou canst love, what art thou? (p. 77)

And immediately he himself gives the answer:

> What art thou? Nothing. In the heart of heart—Nothing. (p. 77)

Bellow here implies that since in his heart of human hearts every man needs to be something, he must seek his identity through the liberating experience of love. But what prevents a man from experiencing; love is the class between 'the pretender soul' and 'the true soul'. While the real soul directs the individual from his true course by substituting vanity for love and social success for genuine self-hood:

> You love a little...give some money to a charity drive. Now that's not love. Is it? What is it? Egotism, pure and simple, it's a way to love the pretender soul. Vanity only vanity is, what it is. And social control. (p. 77)

The pretender soul thus comes to dominate the real soul and the individual becomes blind. This prevents him from the attainment of an authentic self-hood. The pretender soul serves society which destroys individuality. The tragedy is that men cannot but come under the domination of the pretender soul and becomes its slave:

> The interest of the pretender soul is the same of the interest of the social life, the society mechanism. This is the main tragedy of human life.... You are not free. Your own betrayer is inside of you and sells you out. You have to obey him like a slave. He makes you work like a horse. (p. 77)

Tamkin finally draws the conclusion while voicing for Bellow that the most destructive result of this clash between the two is that it is the true soul which has to pay the price:

> The true soul is the one that pays the price. It suffers and gets sick, and it realizes that the pretender can't be loved. Because the pretender is a life. The true soul loves the truth.... Biologically, the pretender soul takes away

> the energy of the true soul and makes it feeble, like a parasite. (p. 78)

Tamkin makes his point clear that by surrendering himself before the demeaning values of the social mechanism, the individual corrupts his life. More than this he makes his chances of redemption narrower.

Thus the enigmatic character of Dr. Tamkin is portrayed with great force by Bellow in so far as the character has a positive role to play in calling forth Wilhelm from death to life. A source of authentic values and healing ideas, Tamkin performs the role of a catalyst in working out the protagonist's transformation by providing him with clues for a true vision of social reality, and of the internal self:

> It was the description of the two souls that had awed him. In Tommy, he saw the pretender. And ever Wilky might not be himself. Might the shame of his true soul be the one by which his grand father had called him—Velvel? (p. 79)

More than this, his awareness of the true self enables him to move in the way of love. He gets in Tamkin what he did not in Dr. Adler:

> That the doctor cared about him pleased him. This was what he craved, that someone should care about him, wish him well. Kindness, mercy, he wanted.

Wilhelm is overwhelmed by the human touch he gets from Tamkin. He now emerges a better and more aware individual from his encounters with this pseudo-psychologist. Despite his hesitation and suspicion concerning the character of his mentor, Wilhelm comes to accept the existential and moral vision put forth by Tamkin. His temporary confusion would come to an end.

Wilhelm moves toward redemption:

> The time must be relinquished. What else could one do about it? Things were too complex, but they might be reduced to simplicity again. Recovery was possible. First, he had to get out of the city. No, first he had to pull out his money.... (p. 85)

Tamkin gradually increases his influence on Wilhelm by his sermons. He hints at the possibilities of Wilhelm, people like whom must face hardship to carry on their existence in the present dehumanized environment. He made it clear that the innocent self must suffer under the immense social pressure. Innocent man desiring to realize the potentialities of his self, more often than not, becomes the victim of the unjust and dehumanized conditioning forces of society. Tamkin strikes at a truth that is applicable not only to Wilhelm, but to all of Bellow's heroes:

> A man like you, humble for life, who wants to feel and live has trouble—not wanting...to exchange an ounce of soul for a pound of social power—he'll never make it without help in a world like this. (p. 86)

He nevertheless assures Wilhelm of success. In his several significant utterances, Tamkin reiterates and amplifies his conviction that man can still manifest his greatness and exercise his capacity for choice and freedom. To achieve this, the individual must liberate his self from the destructive and life corroding demands of money oriented social context and dedicates it to the meaningful fulfillment of its authentic inner needs. Tamkin thus helps Wilhelm to be free of the guilt of his past mistakes and restore his capacity for love, affirmation and fulfillment:

> There's hope for you. You don't really want to destroy yourself...seventy percent of this country is committing suicide by alcohol. Another three may be narcotics. Another sixty just fading away into dust by boredom. Twenty more who have sold their souls to the Devil. Then there's a small percentage of those who want to live. That's the only significant thing in the whole world of today. (p. 107)

Such utterances are significant in view of the affirmative stance taken by Bellow. In Wilhelm too, Bellow manifests this urge to continue life. Even on the verge of destruction he wants to affirm life. Because death is the abolition of choice he wants to retain the freedom to exercise his choice and with all his mistakes, he wants to continue his life. Because life is the supreme value in a Bellow novel to be embraced by man if his existence is to be fulfilled:

> It is the sustaining power of love—that vital emotional base—to carry his peculiar burden, to feel shame and importance, to taste these quelled tears—the only business, the highest business was being done. Maybe the making of mistakes expressed the very purpose of his life and the essence of his being here. Maybe he was supposed to make them and suffer from them on this earth. And though he had raised himself above Mr. Pearls and his father because they adored money still they were called to act energetically and this was better than to yell and cry, pray and beg, poke and blunder and go by fits and starts and fall upon the thorns of life. (pp. 62-63)

Financially crippled and an utter material failure, Wilhelm still considers himself above his father and the like. He still retains his inner dignity that implies the nobility of his self. Bellow thus manifests that the genuine human self like that of Wilhelm is capable of genuine emotions and of a self transcending love. And as Bellow makes his heroes discover the final truth by falling back on his own inner resources, so also Wilhelm discovers the existence of a larger body from which one cannot separate oneself. He even experiences a moment of loving unity with those crowds that formerly made his soul shrink. Bellow is explicit here that only love can affect such a transformative and ennobling vision:

> 'Sin No More' and 'Do Not Eat the Pig' he had particularly noticed. And in the dark tunnel, in the haste heat and darkness which disfigure and make freaks and fragments of nose and eyes and teeth, all of a sudden unsought, a general love for all these imperfect and lurid looking people burst out in Wilhelm's breast. He loved them. One and all, he passionately loved them. They were his brothers and sisters. He was imperfect and disfigured himself, but what difference did that make if he was united with them by this blaze of love? (p. 92)

Wilhelm's feeling of oneness with other human beings implies his acceptance of man's limitations and his sub-angelic position. For a Bellow hero, truth is simple and one's imagination helps in discovering such truths. Time and again, Bellow has stressed that truth is the matter of imagination and not of the intellect. Through the affirmative attitude that enables Wilhelm feel for the human, Bellow shows that it is still possible to retain nobility and continue life in its true dignity even amongst the lonely crowd of a dehumanized modern city environment.

The ending of the novel, which marks Wilhelm's transformation to be complete, is as usual in Bellow, ambiguous. Assuring success of his investment Tamkin advises Wilhelm to practise his 'here-and-now' mental exercise which "stops you from thinking so much about the future and the past and cuts down confusion". And demonstrating the validity of this truth, Tamkin cheats Wilhelm. While he urges him to seize the 'here-and-now', he asks Wilhelm to help a blind, old man across the street and vanishes with Wilhelm's last seven hundred dollars, never to appear again. The words with which Tamkin finally leaves him to his fate are tinged with comic and irony:

> This minute is another instance of the 'here-and-now'. You have to live in this very minute and don't want to. A man asks you for help. Don't think of the market. It won't run away. (p. 109)

Thus Tamkin's philosophy of 'here-and-now' is acted out at the expense of Wilhelm's financial collapse. He is left alone to collapse. He is left alone to compensate his complete financial ruin. Superficially his vision of truth, hope and brightness seem to fail completely. While after investing his last dollars with Tamkin (p. 104). Wilhelm considered him to be on Tamkin's back and resolved that he must 'take the ride' (p. 105), now senses some foul play and tears almost come to his eyes (p. 113). He now realizes that it was not he but Tamkin who was on his back (p. 115). On the verge of collapse he would not get the least sympathy from his father and leave his search of Tamkin.

His search for Tamkin thrusts him into a funeral procession which he soon finds himself in. 'Stripped and kicked out', Wilhelm at once forgets Tamkin. Suddenly he begins to cry for the dead man, another human creature. This feeling of oneness with humanity fulfils his quest and works out a release that undoubtedly bears a universal significant:

> Standing a little apart, Wilhelm began to cry. He cried at first softly and from sentiment, but soon from deeper feelings.... A man—another human creature, was what first went through his thoughts, but other and different things were torn from him. (p. 127)

The 'great knot of ill and grief' in Wilhelm's throat bursts and he cries uncontrollably. These are cries of piercing insight affecting a release making him feel ecstasy: "Soon he was past words, past reason, coherence" (p. 127).

Bellow once again makes his stance clear that hero must enter the world as a simple creature giving up his own ideal construction of self and reality. Only then he can join humanity, not necessarily surrendering to society. The dead one not being any of his relation as the others think to be, it is the inner nobility of Wilhelm's self that urges him, a human creature has a bond with everyone. This is the bond of love, the feeling of which has been his hearts' ultimate need. It is a moment of ecstasy for Wilhelm:

> The flowers and lights fused ecstasically in Wilhelm's blind, wet eyes; the heavy sea-like music came upto his ears. It poured into him where he had hidden himself in the center of a crowd by the great and happy oblivion of tears. He heard it and sank deeper than sorrow, through torn sobs and cries toward the consummation of his heart's ultimate need. (p. 128)

By making his hero cry for another human creature, Bellow again manifests that it is the love for mankind that brings the hero ultimately back to the world, initially repelled by the chaotic and destructive reality. In the present novel, Bellow has worked out this by a greater affirmation of the self through its lies of love with a 'larger body'. Wilhelm has been able to transcend his personal grief by destroying completely his pretender soul. There is now the possibility of communion in place of alienation. He cries for himself and for humanity. He cries for them who are born and who must die. It is a rebirth for Wilhelm which enables him to accept not only his mortality as a man, but also his potentialities as such.

Notwithstanding such an interpretation of the final scene of the novel, Bellow manifests through it that living activity itself is a value. Wilhelm is now aware of the supreme value of life—existence beyond the assessment of financial success or failure. It may be temporary in the scene that Wilhelm will have to continue his struggle for his existence, especially when he has lost his last seven hundred dollars. But as a new self is born with the death of his older one, one can hope that Wilhelm will now be able to cope with his own temperament and the world around him with more ability. It also implies a gesture of love toward life on his part. If 'his heart's ultimate need' is to manifest love, it also urges him to have a commitment to life. He wants to live. The destructive impact of money and brutalities of city life have not killed his heart.

Wilhelm now feels integrity of his identity and thus establishes a communion with humanity itself without submitting before the corrupting influences of society. It makes him aware of his limitations as a human being while implying that man is not merely a part of society, but also a significant tiny part of the greater cosmic order. Bellow never fails to emphasize the role played by love in urging man to continue his life as a true human being with dignity.

Reference

Bellow, Saul, *Seize the Day* (New York, 1965). Subsequent references in parentheses are to this edition.

6

Henderson the Rain King

In *Henderson the Rain King* (1959) things got worse and worse and pretty soon they were too complicated. Chief among the things that become worse are Henderson's social and family relationships. His first marriage to a socially prominent woman ended in divorce, and his second, to a divorcee named Lily Simmons, is aggravated by Henderson's extravagant temperament. Although possessed of three million dollars and a master's degree from an Ivy League university, Henderson's styles himself a boon. He was a bully in his childhood, he assures us, and a wearer of gold earrings in college for the express purpose of provoking fights. Now fifty-five years old he has turned the gentleman's form he inherited from his father into a massive piggery pigs in the elegant stables, pigs in the ornamental gardens, pigs lolling in the drives. He adorns his colossal form with a red velvet bathrobe and filthy boots and strides about his ancestral demesne like a bedlamite, plagued by a voice, within that keeps saying, 'I want, I want, I want'! He has little clue as to what he wants. In a vague intuition that Africa might hold the secret, he accepts, the invitation of a friend named Charlie Albert to accompany him and his bride to the Dark Continent. As a symbol of his commitment, he buys a one-day ticket.

In Africa, Henderson breaks almost immediately with the Alberts, who see themselves as mere tourists, and hires a native guide named Romilayu to take him deep into the country. There he lives briefly with two tribes. The first the cattle loving Arnewi, are suffering from a drought out because of a tribal taboo they will not allow their cattle to drink from a reservoir that has been infested with frogs. Henderson is enchanted by the meekness of Arnewi and by what he conceives to be the wisdom of their queen, Willatale. In a burst of altruism he offers to rid the reservoir of frogs by setting off an explosive in the water. The explosion wrecks the reservoir as well as killing the frogs, and when the Arnewi refuses to kill him for this blunder, Henderson moves on with Romilayu, further into the heart of darkness.

The second tribe Henderson lives with, the lion-obsessed Wariri, are more resourceful than the Arnewi and organize rain ceremonies to deal with the drought. Once again, Henderson cannot resist giving aid: when the tribal man is unable to lift a wooden idol at the ceremonies, Henderson succeeds and thereby becomes the Rain King. He also becomes a friend and admirer of the tribal King, Dahfu, who speaks English and has completed two years of medical school in Beirul before ascending his throne. Henderson especially admires Dahfu's spiritual capacities, which Dahfu claims to draw from a lioness named Atti that he keeps in subterranean captivity. He suggests that Henderson can develop the same capacities. To that end, he encourages him to visit and touch the lion, even to imitate its roar and physical movements. Shortly thereafter, Dahfu is killed in a ritualistic hunt for another lion that is alleged to embody the spirit of his father. Convinced a palace revolution is in process and that he will be named the next king, Henderson flees with Romilayu. In returning to America, he takes with him a lion cub believed by the Wariri to contain the reincarnated spirit of Dahfu.

Henderson who flees Africa is in some ways a changed man, although critics often insist that he is not a changed fundamentally. The voice that has said, 'I want'! for so long, now says, 'She wants, he wants, they want!' Resolved to be a better husband to Lily and father to his five children, and determined to embark on the medical education he has dreamed of for years, he reconnects himself as a young man. More substantially, he connects himself in the last pages of the novel to an orphan boy travelling alone by aeroplane that takes him to America. The boy functions as a mirror of Henderson's own alienation, and when the plane stops for refueling in Newfound land, he and the boy disembark and cavort in the frozen wastes in what seems euphoria of self-realization and acceptance.

Henderson the Rain King is the story of Eugene Henderson and his becoming a rain king. The first non-Jewish hero of Bellow, Henderson enjoys certain advantages of life not accorded to his earlier heroes. He is millionaire of Anglo-saxon protestant stock and suffers none of the outward victimizations of earlier Bellow heroes. Materially affluent Henderson, nevertheless, suffers from a spiritual loneliness. He has a voice within him that ceaselessly says:

> I want, I want...a ceaseless voice in my heart that said, I want, I want, I want, oh I want—yes, go on, I said to myself. Strike, strike, strike, strike. (*HRK*, p. 12)

Despite his being grand financial success, his self in the modern American environment remains dissatisfied and feels a sense of deep frustration—he feels out of place:

> No body truly occupies a station in life any more. There are mostly people who feel that they occupy the place that belongs to another by rights. There are displaced persons every where. (p. 34)

Henderson cannot have a sense of contentment because of his inner voice, which of course admits several interpretations. His inner voice makes his soul restless in the urban mechanized environment:

> America is so big and everybody is working, making, digging, bulldozing, trucking, loading and so on, and I guess the sufferers suffer at the same rate. Everybody wanting to pull together, I tried every cure you can think of. Of course, in an age of madness to expect to be untouched by madness is a form of madness. But the pursuit of sanity can be a form of madness too. (p. 25)

As will be revealed, it is not merely his frustration and feeling of displacement arising out of society's madness that turns him into a questing figure and drives him to the Africa of his soul in pursuit of sanity. The deep voice within him which says, "I want, I want" must be satisfied and this can be satisfied only in a state of isolation away from society itself. He gradually feels that he cannot resist any more, because,

> Things got worse and worse and worse—and pretty soon they were too complicated. (p. 3)

He suffers from a dangling state like that of Joseph or from temporary confusion like that of Wilhelm. His aim is to discover some basic truths about the self and its destiny in a modern environment. But here nobody has a sense of station in life any more. As such, his materially affluent condition would not allow him to have life's wisdom. His temporary confusion can only be ended during his sojourn in his mental Africa where he can get the answer to the persistent cry of his soul. Through the rediscovery of his self, he can discover order and meaning out of chaos and can come to terms with society.

But to know to relate himself to other people, man must first know who he is. Despite Henderson's boasting to his wife Lily that "I am on damned good terms with reality" (p. 36) he will later rightly perceive that he is not yet ready for society. Only after he completes his successful voyage to Africa that he can be ready for meaningful participation in society. More than this he may even come to acquire a sense of belonging—of feeling oneness with humanity. It is love that makes such transformation possible in a Bellow hero and from this point of view; Henderson's quest is for love that can finally redeem his self.

Henderson starts for Africa that "looks like the original place" (p. 47), where he expects to learn "deeper facts of life" (p. 54). As soon as he steps his first step in the land of Arnewi, the tribe he first meets in Africa, he senses a kind of affinity with the pre-human past. It is not in human society but away from it, that the Bellow hero's process of rediscovery of his self starts. The humanist Bellow hero, as hinted earlier, is not yet ready for society. This is the first step he makes in order to remove his deficiency:

> I was still not ready for society. Society is what beats me. Alone I can be pretty good, but let me go among people and there's devil to pay. (p. 49)

Prince Itelo takes him to be a friend and introduces him to the queen Willatale, the grand old woman of the tribe—the woman of Bittahness. Henderson cannot at once answer the question asked by the queen, concerning his identity and the purpose of the visit. He reflects:

> Who—who was I? A millionaire wanderer and way farer. A brutal and violent man driven into the world. A man who fled his own country, settled by his forefathers. A fellow whose heart said, I want, I want. Who played the violin of angels. Who had to burst the spirits' sleep.... (p. 77)

It is important to bear in mind that it is his heart which says "I want, I want". One can also hope that his spirit's sleep can be burst only when his desire is satisfied. In any case, he is touched by the hearty behaviour of the tribes people, which makes his self move toward simplicity and ease. He feels that only living in such simplicity can change a man for the better. This has already done something good to him and while in the huge embrace of the queen, he moves another step forward in his quest:

> ...but suffering is about the only reliable burster of spirit's sleep. There is a rumour long standing that love also does it. (p. 78)

And as he realizes later:

> Between human beings there are only two alternatives, either brotherhood or crime. (p. 80)

Henderson comes to realize that love is the only anti-dote to isolation. Bellow is explicit here in making his stance clear that it is not suffering which one must cherish as a possible way of salvation, but equally important even stronger is the power of love enabling one to burst spirit's sleep. Only love enables one to unlock one's imprisoned self. The wisdom he gains from the queen aids him in unlocking his imprisoned self. He moves toward his rebirth. When the queen later reveals to him that he is a man in love with life, "Gruntu-Molani Men want to live" (p. 85). Henderson discovers another clue to his quest, "What's the best way to live," (p. 81) that the best way to live is for and with other human beings. Goodness is achieved in the company of other men. It is the expression of love:

> Yes, yes, yes: Molani. Me molani. She sees that? God will reward her, tell her, for saying it to me. I'll reward her myself. I'll annihilate and blast those frogs clear out of that Cistern, sky high, they'll wish had never come down from the anountains to bother you. Not only I molani for myself, but for everybody. I could not bear how sad things have become in the world and so I set out because of this molani, Grun-tu-molani, old lady—old queen. Grun-tu-molani, everybody! (p. 85)

This overwhelmed responsible chord struck by the queen's revelation urges Henderson to take some practical steps to drive away the frogs from the cistern. He is caught by the "service motive" and wants to perform an act of love with a firm faith in his potentialities:

> In a crisis a man must be prepared to stand alone, and actually standing alone is the kind of thing I'm good at. (p. 107)

As it were, his enthusiastic application of the modern scientific device not only drives the frogs away, but also the whole water in the cistern. American technology and inventiveness thus prove fatal to his love. Henderson laments:

> Why for once, just once couldn't I get my heart's desire? I have to be doomed always to bungle. (p. 111)

His heart's desire is love, through which he can have his identity as a human being in meaningful participation with other human beings. By destroying the last grain of hope, Henderson cannot share life with the Arnewi. He is dissatisfied and his journey remains incomplete.

For Bellow human life has meaning and it needs to be continued. Bellow in his novels has repeatedly asserted that human life must be continued with all its follies and miseries. A man in love with life like Henderson has to continue his living with all his mistakes accepting limitations:

> And remembering the frogs and many things...thinking of my shame and ruin, but a man goes on living and living things are either better or worse to fellow. This will never stop, and all survivors know it. And you don't die of a trouble somehow you begin to convert it—make use of it, I mean. (p. 114)

Henderson comes to represent all survivors who want to exist in the face of death. To Bellow this urge for survival is itself a manifestation of love. Because he cannot change reality, man must try to make positive use of his failures. His aim has to be the transformation of suffering into joy of living. Bellow implies that merely cherishing suffering does not accord true human stature to a man. He must learn to outlive pain and convert it into joy that urges him to continue existence. Conversely, a man can transform his trouble into joy only when he wants to continue his life as a human being. Human life being a mixture of good and evil is after all a mystery. To live this life meaningfully, one must accept one's limitations—one's sub-angelic position. This implies man's feeling oneness with humanity.

Henderson blows open the cistern when he meant blast out the frogs only. In a need of a community in which he can do some good if his act makes him a kind of schlemiel here, it also makes a point of advance in his attempt to move from becoming to being as will be revealed by his encounter with Dahfu, the chief of the Warriri tribe. Coming voluntarily to the aid of the Arnewi, it is for the first time that he has performed an act for someone else other than himself. He is learning "the best way to live". Despite his failure, he acts as human and asserts his own humanity. Significantly, what his misguided act implies is that suffering is also a part of the learning process of man. Most important, Henderson does express his basic decency in his desire to be a good man in that he takes the constructive action to help the Arnewi and thus expressing his innate desire to live for something other than himself, which act implies his longing to embrace humanity.

In his journey "to see essentials, only essentials, nothing but essentials", he next comes into contact with the Warriri tribe. The chief Dahfu who soon befriends him further unfolds some 'essentials' to Henderson. His insight is further illuminated by Dahfu and it helps Henderson to come up with a clearer vision of himself and the world. Dahfu appears as the teacher and healer to Henderson who can hope to get a measure of cure to his spiritual malaise in prehuman society because the human society cannot provide it to him. Interestingly enough, the savage Dahfu in whom, Hinderson fed up with civilization, seeks wisdom, heals him with the wisdom brought back from civilization. For king Dahfu is a product of Beirut medical school and he does not offer any tribal teaching to Henderson. As Henderson rightly perceives in the very first encounter. Dahfu is already a Being people in contrast to Henderson who is a Becoming one (p. 160).

Henderson laments before the king that while the king is already a Be-er, he himself has miles yet to go to Be:

> King I am a Becomer...you are a Be-er. I've just got to stop Becoming. Jesus Christ, when am I going to Be? (p. 191)

Dahfu recognizes that Henderson is an 'avoider' who cannot live with the knowledge of his inevitable death. He, therefore, develops a plan for him. When by lifting the statue, Henderson becomes the sungo—the rain king, their relation goes to be more intimate. The process of Henderson's move from Becoming to Being continues which can he complete only when he gets the illumination which he has been waiting for. Only then he can find order and meaning for which he has been yearning.

It is becoming evident that it is Dahfu by his healing ideas helps Henderson to have his desired illumination. Dahfu plans the recovery of Henderson by bringing him face to face with death. Coming before the lioness Atti, Henderson again remembers the prophecy Daniel made to king Nebuchadnezzar. He first felt this while raising pigs. Indeed, he feels drawn to animal kingdom more and less to human society. He is not ready to join society as yet:

> Once again I brought to mind that old prophecy Daniel made to Nebuchadnezzar. They shall drive thee from among men, and thy dwelling shall be with the beast of the field. The lion odor was still very keen on my fingers. I smelled it repeatedly and there returned to my thoughts the frogs of Arnewi, the cattle...the tenant's cat...to say nothing of the pigs I had bred. Sure enough the prophecy has a peculiar relevance for me, implying perhaps that I was not entirely fit for companionship. (pp. 229-30)

Despite his feeling of his unfitness for human companionship, his being brought into contact with the lioness by Dahfu teaches him something significant. Henderson now learns that man must accept death. He must learn to continue his life by accepting his limitations. Only then he can qualify himself to join humanity which in turn enables him to have his true dignity as a human being. Henderson, who wanted to see, "if human kind cannot stand much reality, how much unreality can it stand?", (p. 105) now learns to humble down before the unchangeable facts of life:

> So I had no business to make terms with life, but had to accept such conditions as it would let me have. (p. 210)

This humbling down marks his rediscovery of self, which now it is capable of accepting life in exact terms. Man must accept his sub-angelic position. By accepting the stature for himself exactly human, he can attempt at the realization of his potentialities to make his meaningful. Henderson now becomes aware that "one should have a suitable image of himself" (p. 286). He moves forward in his way of finding wisdom of life. Bellow artistically connects this with the nature of American civilization which has committed itself to restless and restless action without any basis for meaningful change. Such change does not result in any viable growth, and as Henderson observes sharing with his creator, that the greatest problem for a nation like America is the courage to face death:

> All the major tasks and the big conquest were done before my time. That left the biggest problem of all, which was to encounter death. We've just got to do something about it. It isn't just me. Millions of

> Americans have gone forth since the war to redeem the present and discover the future. I can swear to you.... And it's the destiny of my generation of Americans to go out in the world and try to find the wisdom of life. (pp. 276-77)

This wisdom of life Henderson learns in one of the moving incident of the novel in which the king Dahfu loses his life. Henderson realizes now that without the spirit of altruism life has no meaning. He also becomes aware of the need of the sacrifice for the community—as the king himself does. He senses a heart-felt need to save the king from imminent death:

> Your majesty, move over and I'll lie beside you. Or else be me and live, I never knew what to do with life any way, and I'll die instead. (p. 312)

This is a clear token of his spiritual rebirth. The clamorous voice that used to say "I want, I want", can now listen to other voices too:

> I had a voice that said, I want. I want? I? It should have told me she wants, he wants, they want. And more over, it's love that makes reality. The opposite makes the opposite. (p. 286)

Identity is achieved in communion and Henderson reaches this communion not in the civilization to which he is born, but out of it. Already having expressed his pride of the ability to suffer, he learns to transform this ability into a capability of all encompassing love. The love that springs in his heart convinces him that "Chaos don't run the whole show" and urges him to "start life anew".

> The only decent thing about me is that I have loved certain people in my life.... If only we didn't have hearts we wouldn't know how sad it was. But we carry around these hearts, this spoty damn mangoes in our breasts, which give us away.... I've gotten to that age where I need human voices and intelligence. That's all that's lift. Kindness and love. (p. 316)

Bellow again reveals his faith in the power of imagination by implying that Henderson's voyage has all along been a mental one. The marvellous revelation that now captures Henderson's heart has occurred in his inner psyche:

> I saw a few things in the interior.... I have had a look into some of the fundamentals. (p. 331)

This delving has enabled him to value human existence—man himself has his principal work of art. He has ceased to become and began to be. His quest fulfilled. Henderson can now have communion with other human beings in meaningful terms—he can be a member of humanity. Being face to face with death he carries its living symbol—the lion cub, symbolizing the wisdom of Dahfu. When his plane lands in Newfoundland, *en route* to New York, for refueling, Henderson finds a stranger child whom he takes to his chest. As the child cannot speak English, obviously their relationship will be an emotional one rather than verbal. He is now not isolated. His alienation has come to an end, as he has acquired a newer vision in his sojourn in mental Africa. He now knows who he is and the world is no longer hostile to him. His inner voice has now reached a state of calmness. Life is now for him a possible source of joy. His return with hope, in fact, is a powerful celebration and all that in positive in life. Like earlier Bellow heroes, Henderson starts as a solitary, fleeing society in search of love and returns with a new sense of hope and joy. He attains a vision that permits him to be in charge of his own fate.

It becomes by now evident that Bellow celebrates life against despair in the present novel. Man is finally defined by human condition. Like other Bellow's heroes, it is the love of mankind that brings back Henderson to the world—to the business of living, even when the real seems chaotic and destructive. By making him accept the sub-angelic position of man, Bellow works out the possibility of fulfilment for his hero in a renewed state, his self gets transformed enabling him to earn a nobler vision that spontaneously draws him to humanity. Bellow hints time and again that such a transformation is possible by the blaze of love and vice versa. Such an illumination is not mere knowledge. It is something more which purifies the human soul and makes its salvation possible.

Reference

Bellow, Saul, *Henderson the Rain King* (Harmondsworth, 1983). Subsequent references in parentheses are to this edition.

7

Herzog

Herzog (1965) is the story of Moses Elkanah Herzog, a twice divorced college professor who reviews his life while living a bachelor existence in his run down house in the hills of western Massachusetts. During the course of the novel, Herzog reviews especially, the five days that have culminated in his return to the Berkshire town of Ludeville and to a house he had abandoned in his defence to his second wife, Madeleine who is now living in Chicago with Valentine Gersbash and Herzog's young daughter Junie. The days revive for Herzog with present tense—immediacy. On day one, he decides to visit his friend Libbie Sissler on Martha's Vineyard in order to evade his mistress, Ramona Donsell, who has an obvious interest in marriage. But as soon as he arrives at the Sisslers he knows he has made a mistake. While supposedly settling in, he decamps again for New York, leaving a note that offers a variety of frantic, half thought excuses. 'Have to go back', he writes:

> Not able to stand kindness at this time. Feeling, heart, everything in strange condition. Unfinished business. Bless you both.

He spends day two partially with Ramona, and on day three he tries to see his lawyer, Harvey Simkin, to learn if he can gain custody of Junie. Having arranged to meet Simkin in a courthouse, he is diverted by a series of hearings in the court, among them the arrangements of an intern who had made a sexual advance to a detective in a man's toilet, of a male transvestite who has attempted to hold up a store with a toy pistol, and of a young mother and her lover who are charged with the murder of her three year-old child. The last of these cases triggers a fear for his own daughter's safety, and he flies immediately to Chicago, where he takes a pistol from his deceased father's home and goes in search of Madeline and her lover with murder in his heart—murder forestalled when he looks through a window and sees Gersbach giving Junie a bath with fatherly tenderness. On day four he arranges to take Junie to the Shedd Aquarium and has a traffic accident, whereupon he is charged with carrying a concealed weapon. After bond is posted by his brother Will, he returns to the Berkshires, and that return on day five brings the novel full circle to its point of departure.

In *Herzog* Bellow depicts, through his hypersensitive intellectual humanist hero Herzog, the chaos of a self in the modern dehumanized environment. His search for freedom has been threatened by a sense of nullity. Already troubled and confused by a mess of ideas, Herzog's consciousness is in collision with the version of reality, both in history and in society around him. Bellow rightly hints at the theme of *Herzog* when he says:

> To me, a significant theme of Herzog is the imprisonment of the individual in a shameful and impotent privacy. He feels humiliated by it, he struggles comically with it, and he comes to realize that what he considered his intellectual privilege has proved to be another form of bondage. Anyone who misses this, misses the point of the book. (*H*, p. 76)

His rich intelligence makes him a scholar of repute. But it comes to mock him, because it cannot provide his self with any universal connections to relieve his sense of misery. In constant search of order and meeting, his soul therefore meets up only with chaos and disorder.

Like earlier Bellow's heroes, Herzog relentlessly struggles to gain a measure of freedom from the conditioning forces of both history and time. His problem is that he cannot cope with a world which appears hostile to his own heart felt vision and his own orderly view. He discovers that facts here are binding and the essentials are lost in the dark. The indignities he has to suffer in such a world cannot subdue him to the surrounding worldly cynicism and he insists on a better fate. He ceaselessly attempts to liberate his self from such decaying forces and makes adventures those occur mainly in his mind.

It is this mind which constrained in interaction with a social universe and is at odds with it. The series of experiences of Bellow's socially maladjusted hero mainly consist of his confrontation with characters who play their roles representing the distractive and distorting forces of society finally leading Herzog to his confused state. While Bellow presents the dichotomy between the private and the civil self through his protagonist, Herzog himself becomes a universal figure in his struggle against the dehumanizing forces and standing as the eternal sentinel for the human and the durable values.

Thus the external reality with which Herzog can hardly come into terms, becomes the external referent for his inner despair. To focus the anguish of Herzog's inner self, Bellow therefore makes his hero undergo a series of experiences both in his private and public realms. Most of these come up with negative results for him. While his private life becomes store house of miseries and misfortunes, in public life, he cannot but quarrel with most of the idea makers of the history past and present. A very significant point to be kept in mind at this stage is that most of the quarrels Herzog gets himself involved in the realm of ideas, are concerned with the dignity of self and human values.

In his private life, he has been twice divorced. His best friend Valentine Gersbach has cuckolded him. His friendships have been failures and most important, he has fallen short of his scholarly ambitions. He has been denied switches in love, sex, philosophy, religion and human relationships. The world for Herzog both internal and external—has become a mighty oppressor. Especially the wreck of his second marriage proves to be fatal for him and the damage caused by it is beyond his endurance. Alienated and frustrated he tries to create order out of personal chaos. But initially he feels displaced—belonging to no where. By depicting the tribulations of his hero and working out a state of release through Catharsis, Bellow in fact puts innocence to test in the face of harsher reality. To attain the state of cleanness, the Bellow's hero must undergo the state of suffering, so also it cannot prevent him from his struggle to achieve dignity and impose a moral dimension upon life.

That, the intellectual Herzog cannot agree with the idea-makers of history, has been mentioned in the Third Chapter. Most of the ideas and problems he wrestles with, have also been come under attack of earlier Bellow's heroes. In fact, Bellow himself has discussed these issues in his numerous articles and essays. Herzog's disagreement is mainly with those propagating nihilistic ideas. But presently his family has been disintegrated and familial relationships have been shattered. He has to face the dreadful impact of money in a mechanized city existence in America, where man Herzog has become money's medium. All this has brought a halt to his scholarly interests. Believing that 'Man's life is not a business', the humanist intellectual Herzog planned a comprehensive history of man-kinds, making account for the disturbed human condition of the present century:

> What he planned was a history which really took into account the revolutions and mass convulsions of the twentieth century accepting with de Tocqueville, the universal and durable development of the quality of conditions, the progress of democracy. (p. 6)

But reality for him has been so brutal that he cannot justify his present existence, let alone continue his scholarly pursuits:

> Considering his entire life, he realized that he has mismanaged everything. His life was...ruined. (p. 6)

He comes to have an ironic look at his intellectual mission which comes to mock him now:

> Herzog smiled at this earlier avatar of his life, at Herzog the victim, Herzog the would be lover, Herzog the man whom the world depended for certain intellectual work to change history, to influence the development of civilization. Several boxes of state paper under his bed in

> Philadelphia were going to produce the very significant result. (pp. 104-05)

Leaving his scholarly pursuits, Herzog nevertheless, attempts to be out of this ruin and to keep his dignity intact. But reality poses as a bottleneck and would not allow an individual to assert his freedom. If he quarrels with the idea-makers of history so also he cannot abide by the reality principles preached by the 'Reality Instructors'. He is aware that he himself is one of them:

> A very special sort of lunatic expects to inculcate his principles. Sandor Himmelstein, Valentine Gensbach, Madeleine, P. Herzog Moses himself, Reality instructors, they want to teach you—to punish you with—the lessons of the real. (p. 125)

One can easily discern from Herzog's relationship with his friends and relatives that these teachings of reality according to their own version have contributed much to the disorientation of his personality. These reality instructors, in fact, with their version of reality, threaten to crush the basic human innocence represented by Herzog. Rather than offering any co-operation in his project, they being the corruptive forces of society prevent his humanistic ideal:

> He appeared to know how everything ought to go down to the smallest detail.... But all he asked, it seemed to him was a bit of co-operation his effort, benefiting everyone to work toward a meaningful life. (p. 123)

It with his humanistic ideal that he started his study presented by abandoned:

> ...his study was supposed to have ended with a new angle on the modern conditions, showing how life could be lived by renewing universal connections, overturning the last of the romantic errors about the uniqueness of the self; revising the old western, Faustion ideology; investing the social meaning of nothingness. (p. 39)

These instances make it evident for any serious reader of Bellow that despite his distance from his protagonist, Bellow has come to profess certain ideas he holds so dear in his heart.

Herzog makes it clear that the idea of the self has undergone significant changes. Man's function now is to discover new areas of potentialities under changed circumstances because man is still capable of realizing his potentialities, despite the fact that "...people can be free now but the freedom does not have any content. It's like a howling emptiness" (p. 39), man has to assert his individuality in the face of nothingness. This is in fact the main issue of contention between Herzog and the reality instructors, both in history and in time.

It was enough to make a man pray to God to remove this great, bone breaking burden of selfhood and self development, and give himself a failure, back to the species for a primitive cure. But this was becoming the up-to-date and almost conventional way of looking at any single life. Everyone was in the act. History gave anyone a free ride. The very Himmelsteins who had never even read a book of metaphysics were touting the void as if it were so much saleable real estate. This little demon was impregnated with modern ideas, and one in particular excited his terrible little heart:

> You must sacrifice your poor squawking niggardly individuality—which may be nothing any way but a persistent, infantile megalomania or a striking little bourgeois property—to historical necessity. And to truth. And truth is true only it brings down more disgrace and deariness upon human beings, so that if it shows anything except evil, it is illusion, and not truth. (pp. 92-93)

In spite of the irony inherent in the utterances, Herzog here echoes his creator and is all serious in clearly opposing the idea of Void and Nothingness propounded in the present century. Through his protagonist, Bellow probably laments that anything that brings down more 'disgrace and dreariness' upon human beings is taken as truth which shows anything except evil is taken to be illusion and not truth. Likewise, Herzog refuses to believe that the modern age is worse than any other and will not endorse pessimism. Such popularization of nihilistic ideas infuriates him. He rages against Heidegger, when he finds him to talk of the fall:

> Dear Doktor Professor Heidegger, I should like to know what you mean by the expression the fall into the quotidian. When did this fall occur? Where were we standing when it happened? (p. 49)

The above instances testify to the fact that for Herzog the potentialities of human life must be perennial. Though there is evil in the world, he refuses to accept it as the soul reality. Most of the ideas offering versions of reality are therefore untenable to him. In contrast to his firm faith in the human potentialities, most of these ideas are life denying. He sees himself in a historical context and is conscious of his role as a responsible guardian of culture and society. He, therefore, takes the burden upon him of correction these misconceptions and fallacies he encounters battles against these ideas with his own. In his attempt to improve the human condition what appears to him as most disturbing is that none of these philosophers has ever taken the pain to talk of ordinary human life. His lamentation betokens the sincerity of his attempt:

> ...very tired of the modern form of historicism which sees in this civilization the defeat of the best hopes of western religion and thought what Heidegger calls the second Fall of Man into quotidian or ordinary. No philosopher knows what the ordinary is, has not fallen into it deeply enough. The question of ordinary human experience is the principal question of these modern centuries, as Mantaige and Pascal, otherwise in disagreement, both clearly saw the strength of a man's virtue or spiritual capacity measured by his ordinary life. (p. 106)

Virtually cut off from the outside world, it is his consciousness that he initiates the battles to restore meaning and order which may finally lead him to sanity. The present inner chaos makes him fly into a rage and he becomes totally alienated. Aware of the inconsistency and fragmentation of a modern individual, he begins to live in his own 'ideal constructions'. With a keen desire to affirm the human against the inhuman elements of the present civilization, he seeks for those values and enduring human qualities, the absence of which make him sick and which for him, are indispensable to make human life a decent one and thus enabling each individual to have true human dignity and complete his life in meaningful terms. Viewed from this stand point, Herzog is a rebel with a cause. His cause is the defense of humanity. At the same time he is also a victim of the conditioning forces of history and time. Herzog rightly perceives that it is values in a devalued materialistic world which are of supreme importance to make human life significant:

> Are all the traditions used up: the beliefs done for, the consciousness of the masses not yet ready for the next development? Is this the full crisis of dissolution? Has the filthy moment come when moral feeling dies, conscience disintegrates, and respect for liberty, law public decency, all the rest collapses in cowardice, decadence, blood? (p. 74)

Here too, Herzog battles against the idea-makers in whom he finds nothing but the hollow intellection, which collides with his own idea of importance of human heart:

> But we must not forget how quickly the visions of genius become the canned goods of intellectuals. The canned Sauer Kraut of Spangler's 'Prussian socialism', the common places of the wasteland outlook the cheap mental stimulants of Alienation, the cant and rant of pips—queaks about. Inauthenticity and Forlonness. I can't accept this foolish dreariness. We are talking about the whole life of mankind. (pp. 74-75)

It is against 'the common places of the wasteland outlook, the cheap mental stimulants of alienation' that Herzog launches his crusade. Himself being an intellectual of repute, he had earlier come to acknowledge the limit of the intellect. He believes that more intellection can provide nothing worthwhile to mankind. It is not enough to explain the complex human phenomenon. Herzog is convinced that human life is far subtler than any of its models. As such he insists on the wedding of the intellect and the imagination. It is only when intellect gets wedded to imagination that some ways of recovery may be discovered. Aware of the fact that the image of the individual self has been turned from 'I or we' into 'It' in a mass society, Herzog repeatedly affirms his faith in the human and believes that the individual self is still with its inherent potentialities:

> In man, self awareness has been accompanied at this stage with a sense of the loss of more general natural powers of a price paid by instinct by sacrifices of freedom, impulse. The drama of this stage of human development seems to be the drama of disease, of self revenge. An age of special comedy. What we see is not simply the leveling de Tocqueville predicted, but the plebein stage of evolutionary self-awareness. Perhaps the revenge taken by numbers, by the species on our impulses of narcissism is inevitable. In this new region of multitudes, self awareness tends to reveal us to ourselves as monsters.... The individual is obliged or put under pressure to define 'power' as it is defined in politics and to work out the personal consequences of this for himself. Thus he is provoked to take revenge upon himself, a revenge of derision, contempt, denial of transcendence. (pp. 163-64)

Herzog admits that the mechanized civilization has lowered the status of individual self previously enjoyed by it. In a letter to General Eisenhower, Herzog analyzes the present condition of the self in a mass-civilization which tends to drive away the 'private life' and where measure of man comes to be taken in terms of Gross National Product contrary to such an idea, Herzog expresses his firm faith in the inner resources of man, that may help one to realize one's potentialities and thus vindicates the worth of the self in the present mechanized environment:

> The more political our society becomes the more individuality seems lost. Seem, I say, because it has millions of secret resources. More plainly, national purpose is now involved with the manufacture of commodities in no essential to human life, but vital to the political survival of the country. Because we are now all sucked into these phenomena of Gross National

> Product, we are forced to accept the sacred character of certain absurdities of falsehoods whose high priests not so long ago were pitchmen and figures of derision...on the other hand there is more private life than a century ago, when the working day lasted fourteen hours. The whole matter is of the highest importance since it has to do with invasion of the private sphere by techniques of exploitation and domination. (pp. 162-63)

It is by now evident that Herzog is serious and also regretful that the mechanized civilization has come to turn the 'I or We' into 'It'. The individual self appears to be meagre in the face of a gigantic influence of a huge technological advancement:

> What it means to be a man. In a city. In a century. In transition. In a mass. Transformed by science. Under organized power. An object to tremendous controls. In a condition caused by mechanization. After the late failure of radical hopes. In a society that was no community and devalued the person. Owing to the multiplied power of numbers which made the self negligible which spent military billions against foreign enemies but would not pay for order at home. Which permitted savagery and barbarism in its own great cities.... The beautiful supermachinery opening a new life for innumerable mankind. (p. 201)

Then again to Herzog, the changes brought forth by the government with technological aid seldom and to human growth. These changes are hardly life-enhancing. The contrary is rather true in that it debarred the individual self:

> To live in an inspired condition to know truth, to be free, to love another, to consummate existence to abide with a death in clarity of consciousness.... (p. 165)

To put the matter in a different way, all such attempts of change are devoid of any interest that can add to make human life meaningful. These do not count values, for which Herzog relentlessly aspires. To Herzog, the most dreadful impact of technology has been that it has not only taken the place of but has come to absorb the human qualities without which no decent human life is possible:

> Intellectual observers have pointed out that 'spiritual' honor or respect formerly reserved for justice, courage temperance, mercy may now be earned in the negative by the grotesque...this development is possibly related to the fact that so much of 'value' has been absorbed by technology itself. It is 'good' to electrify a primitive area. Civilization and even morality are implicit in technological transformation. Isn't it good to give bread to the hungry, clothe to the naked? Don't we obey Jesus in shipping machinery to Peru or Sumatra? Good is easily done by machines of production and transformation, can virtue complete. (p. 164)

While swallowing up all virtues and qualities from human life, the prevalent general faith on the power of technology has contributed toward devaluing of human life. Man at present is not Man, but a mere creature:

> Perhaps...people wish life to end. They have polluted it. Courage honour, frankness, friendship, duty, all made filthy. Sullied. So that we loathe the daily bread that prolongs useless existence. There was a time when men were born, lived and died. But do you call these men? We are only creatures. (p. 133)

It is no wonder that Herzog here comes nearest to Bellow who also raises almost the same question regarding the power of human qualities in relation to the power of technology in one of his articles and comes up with his conviction in the power of inner resources of a man which only can help in discovering human qualities and leads him to a meaningful life through the recovery of his inner health:

> The virtues which make such meaningful life possible need not be sought for in the outer world. These are not to be invented but to be discovered. Because these are there deep within one's own heart. The only need is to restore values which make the rediscovery. But the value as I see it is not one of definite but of the total reconsideration of human qualities. Or perhaps, even the

> discovery of qualities. I am certain that there are human qualities still to be discovered. (p. 164)

There are positive and clear hints in Herzog's utterances that the formulations which hamper such discovery must be wiped out or at least, be modified. While attaching importance to one's own inner resources, Herzog feels the urgent need of a total reconsideration of these formulations so as to enable the individual self a life based on dignity:

> Such discovery or recovery is only hampered by definitions which hold mankind down at the level of pride asserting too much and then suffering from self hatred as consequences. (p. 164)

Herzog tells us:

> Much of my life has been spent in the effort to live by more coherent ideas. (p. 164)

He tries to get hold of these 'coherent ideas' of his own because it is evident by now, he loves life and wants to survive as a human being against all the oddities of a modern existence. Like earlier Bellow's hero, Herzog also comes to express his faith in the ennobling power of suffering, but what he insists on, is that to experience this, one must possess the desire to exist. In this point, he is in agreement with Neitzschi.

> I also know you think that deep pain is ennobling pain which burns slow, like green wood, and there you have me with you, somewhat. But for this higher education survival is necessary. You must out live the pain. (p. 319)

In consonance with such ideas expressed by Herzog, one can convincingly hold that it is his desire for survival—his love for life that urges him to continue life and leads him toward the recovery of his mental health:

> ...the first requirement of stability in a human being was that the said human being should really desire to exist. This is what Spinoza says. It is necessary for happiness. He cannot behave well or live well if he himself doesn't want to live. (p. 96)

While Herzog suffers the pangs of a dehumanized world, his suffering gradually performs its task of ennobling his soul. Bellow does not make his heroes luxuriate in suffering. Rather he uses it as a device for working out a transformation of his protagonists. Herzog makes it explicit while he refers to Kierkegaard:

> I venture to say Kierkegaard meant that truth has lost its force with us and horrible pain and evil must teach it to us again, the eternal punishments of Hell will have to regain their reality before mankind turns serious once more...let us set aside the fact that such convictions in the mouths of safe, comfortable people playing at crisis, alienation, apocalypse and desperation, make me sick. We must get it out of our heads that this is a doomed time that we are walking for the end, and at the rest of it.... But, to get to the main point, the advocacy and praise of suffering take us in the wrong direction and those of us who remain loyal to civilization must not go for it. You have to have the power to employ pain, to repent, to be illuminated. You must have the opportunity and even the time. With the religious, the love of suffering is a form of gratitude to experience or an opportunity to experience evil and change it into good. (pp. 316-17)

Herzog acknowledges in clear terms the tempering effect of suffering as an important ingredient of man's transformation and salvation. It is his ability to employ suffering in the right direction that enables him to outlive pain and in a sense to come to terms with reality. It has its soothing effect and renders a healing touch to the malaise of his psyche, hence his calming down and advancing toward sanity. It works out finally a transformation:

> ...people of powerful imagination, given to dreaming deeply and to raising up marvelous and self sufficient fictions, twin to suffering sometime to cut into their bliss, as people pinch themselves to feel awake. I know that my suffering...has often been like that, a more and an antidote to illusion, and therefore I can take no moral

> credit for it. I am willing without further exercise in pain to open my heart. (p. 317)

Thus suffering for the Bellow's hero has been a more extended form of life, a striving for true wakefulness and Herzog comes to his complete wakefulness through it. His wish to open his heart marks the starting point of the rediscovery of his self. He is moving to sanity:

> And this needs no doctrine or theology of suffering. We love apocalypses too much, and crisis ethics and florid extremism with its thrilling language.... I've had all the monstrosity I want. We've reached on again the history of mankind when we can ask about certain persons: "What is this thing"? No more of that for me no, no: I am simply a human being, more or less. (p. 317)

Herzog thus out of his struggles and manages himself to exist. This struggle, containing man's intellectual, emotional and spiritual spheres, against doom seems to be inherent in the human condition. Encompassing wonder as well as suffering, this struggle has a metaphysical dimension. Herzog himself makes it clear that this realization this humbling down has come to him from his within—not from any constructs of the intellect:

> ...I have been spared the chief ambiguities that afflicts intellectuals hate and resent the civilization that makes their lives possible. What they love is an imaginary human situation invented by their own genius and which they believe is the only true and the only human reality. How odd. (p. 304)

Contrary to such ideas what one can hold is that it is the innate power of his own self that makes this new awareness possible. The human phenomenon is vaster and more complex than any meaning man can assign to it. The ambitious models of life provided by the reality instructors are caricature of the real thing, as they cannot see the obvious. Herzog now attains a newer vision. He is more clear what it means to be a human and how should a good man live.

While working out such a state of calmness for his protagonist, Bellow has all along stressed the human element in Herzog. In contrast to the sense of the void propagated by the nihilists, and which Herzog has relentlessly been fighting with, he all along conforms to the idea of meaning of human life. He stresses his firm faith in humanity which as an intellectual he tries to rejuvenate by his scholarly writings. In pursuit of a grand synthesis, he wants to give history a newer interpretation. He resists with his all humanitarian outlook, the differing systems by which other people account for the way reality is. He rather wants a system that may eventually make each individual life a meaningful one. To effect such a change, Herzog believes, no outward remedy would do any good. It must originate in each heart, wherein springs love:

> ...whether justice on this earth can or cannot be general, social, but must orginate within each heart. Subjective monstrosity must be overcome, must be corrected by community, by useful duty. (p. 219)

But to achieve such a state, Herzog believes, that there should be a change of heart, without which no meaning could perhaps be assigned to individual life. He repeatedly asserts that there must be a change of heart only which could free man of the depressive ideas. For Herzog, love has the power to effect such a change. He makes a fervent appeal:

> The point was that there were people who could destroy mankind and that they were foolish and arrogant, crazy and must be begged not to do it. Let the enemies of life step down. Let each man now examine his heart, I would not trust myself in a position of authority. (p. 51)

Herzog, the intellectual and humanist comes to defend humanity against all the apocalyptic ideas preached throughout history. In fact, Bellow makes explicit his own belief in such a change of heart by hinting at the need of such a change in *Herzog*. While the court scene strikes a point of change in him, it makes him witness the brutalities engineered by a corrupt civilization. His human feelings remain dumb and powerless while witnessing the child-murder case:

> With all his might and heart he tried to obtain something for the murdered child. But what? How? He pressed himself with intensity but all his might could get nothing for the buried boy. Herzog experienced nothing but his own human feelings.... What if he felt moved to cry? Of pray? He pressed hand to hand. And what did he feel? Why he felt himself—his own trembling hands and eyes that stung. And what was there in modern, post...post Christian America to pray for? Justice—justice and mercy? And pray away the monstrousness of life, the wicked dream it was? He opened his mouth to relieve the pressure he felt. He was wrung, and wrung again, and wrung again, again. (p. 204)

What is this if not love and humanity? Like Herzog, Bellow has been persistent in defending humanity. By identifying him with the dead child, Herzog accepts his own mortality and symbolically joins the oppressed humanity. The brutalities he does witness in the court, urges him to see his daughter Junie, presently living with Gersbach and Madeleine. He becomes afraid lest Gersbach should do any harm to his little Junie and rushes to Chicago with dead father's pistol. He decides to shoot Gersbach if he has done anything wrong to his daughter. But contrary to his expectation, what he sees is, Gersbach bathing Junie with all care and tenderness:

> As soon as Herzog saw the actual person giving an actual bath, the reality of it, the tenderness of such a buffoon to a little child, his intended violence turned into theater, into something ludicrous. He was not ready to make such a complete fool of himself. Only self hatred could lead him to ruin himself because his heart was 'broken'.... His breath came back to him, and how good it felt is breathe. (p. 258)

Despite the grotesqueness of Gersbach it is an act of love which he performs. It is a holy act that touches Herzog's heart. While the court scene has a role to play in bringing Herzog to Chicago, it is his observance of his bathing scene that marks the actual point of his moving toward health. The moment he decides not to shoot Gersbach is the crucial—moment of

Herzog's progress from sickness to health. It works but the final catharsis in him. Herzog can now start his life anew: "He must live complete his assignment, whatever that was" (p. 231). He feels good to breathe love.

Herzog's recovery is complete. He has stopped thinking. Even his intellectual pursuits—mere abstractions—cannot interest him now in view of his newer illumination:

> ...he realized that he did not need to perform elaborate abstract intellectual work—he had always thrown in himself into as if it were the struggle for survival. But not thinking is not necessarily fatal. Did I really believe that I would die when thinking stopped? Now to fear such a thing—that's really crazy. (p. 232)

Herzog wants to continue with his mysterious existence regardless of the void. He feels and experiences a sense of deep contentment that his consciousness had not been swept away by the versions of the theorists. He has learnt to survive these idiocies:

> Luckily for me, I didn't have the means to get too far a way from our common life. I am glad of that. I mean to share with other human beings as far as possible and not destroy my remaining years in the same way. Herzog felt a deep, dizzy, eagerness to begin. (p. 322)

This deep, dizzy, eagerness to begin makes him further move from the realm of ideas. Rather, it is his interest in the ordinary life that makes him aware of the interest power residing in each individual soul:

> The necessary premise is that a man is some how more than his 'characteristics', all the emotions, strivings tastes and constructions which it pleases him to call 'My life'. We have ground to hope that a life is something more than such a cloud of particles, mere facticity. Go through what is comprehensible and you conclude that only the incomprehensible gives any light. (p. 256)

Herzog therefore rejects the versions of the theoreticians who come to profess mere 'potato love'. Human life is far subtler than any of its models. As such Herzog does place his faith in the power of human soul. Only where from can one expect to get at truth. Rationalistic approach to life is incapable of rendering meaning to the human life:

The dream of man's heart however much we may distruct and resent it, is that life may complete itself in significant pattern. Some incomprehensible way. Before death. Not irrationally, but incomprehensibly fulfilled. Spared by these clumsy police guardians, you get one last chance to know justice. Truth. (p. 303)

Although interested in socio-political questions, what Herzog seeks for life is neither a philosophical nor a social pattern. He seeks for a significant pattern which will be simply incomprehensible beyond any formulation of mind and language. To achieve such a pattern Herzog implies, would be to escape all visible patterns that constitute modern life. Obviously then, there is something mystical about the pattern of life. Herzog seeks for.

It is evident that Herzog aspires for must be based on values. As is to be expected, therefore, Herzog wants in the main, restoration of values which have been devalued by 'Skeptics' in each generation. Life based on values can attain meaning which spontaneously urges each individual, it is implied to share his life with other individuals. Again, it is the manifestation of an all encompassing love:

> We must help one another. In this irrational world, where mercy, compassion, heart, all rare things hard won in many human battle fought by rare minorities, victories whose results should never be taken for granted, for they were seldom reliable in any one—rare things, were often debunked, renounced repudiated by every generation of skeptics. Reason itself, logic, urged you to kneel and give thanks for every small sign of true kindness. (p. 199)

Herzog's spiritual rebirth has made this sort of realization possible for him enabling him to feel a bond of oneness with the entire humanity.

With his renewed faith in God, Herzog has now learnt how a good man should live. He is now aware that identity is found in communion through love. The feeling of love urges him to make his life meaningful in brotherhood:

> I really believe that brotherhood is what makes a man human. If I owe God a human life, this is where I fall down. Man lived not by self alone but in his brother's face.... Each shall be hold the Eternal. Father and love and joy abound. When the preachers of dead tell you that others only distract you from metaphysical freedom then you must turn away from them. The real and essential question is one of our employment by other human beings and their employment by us. Without this true employment you never dread death, you cultivate it. And consciousness when it does not clearly understand what to live for, what to die for, can only abuse and ridicule itself. (pp. 272-73)

Herzog makes it evident that the dream of his heart has been that life may complete itself in a significant pattern. One can now hold that this pattern consists of a mystical bond of brotherhood among human beings. By this Herzog expresses his disavowal of self-centredness and a spontaneous flow of establishing meaningful relationships of mutual responsibility. An unprecedented calm visits his consciousness and hence his eagerness to begin.

Herzog's alienation has come to an end. In discovering the meaning of what it means to be human, he has rediscovered his self and its true meaning and purpose. As hinted earlier, his resolution is completely internal. Although his resolution does not make him initiate any of his good intentions, it marks the end of sickness and a promise of cure. It is Herzog's joyous sanity—the other side of suffering. There will be no more insistent intellectualization nothing of the sort. He has attained a state of sweet reasonableness. Accepting limitations, he has learnt to submit. Now he is content to be:

> Anyway, can I pretend I have much choice? I look at myself and see chest, things, feet—a head. This strange organization, I know it will die. And inside something,

> happiness.... Thou movest me. Something produces intensity, a holy feeling...some hearts put out more love and some less of it, presumably.... My face too blind, my mind too limited, my instincts too narrow. But this intensity, doesn't it mean anything?... But that is just it —not a solitary thing. I am pretty well satisfied to be just as it is willed, and for as long as it I may remain in occupancy. (p. 340)

Herzog's affirmation is not a fraud—not a cheap one. He has endured alienation. A victim of anguish and nausea, he has experienced the void in all its terror. Herzog's innocence is 'the radi-innocence' (Ihab Hassan) that reasserts itself against negation. By his final celebration of feeling and brotherhood, Herzog rejects the void—because it lacks a heart.

Bellow thus shows that to celebrate life, one must accept limitations and join humanity. Only then can a man discover his true identity. His true identity consists of the fact that he is a tiny part of the mysterious larger body. Such a feeling renders him the sense of dignity as an individual. To put the matter in a different way, his quest for self gets itself satisfied only when he returns to community. The struggle of the self to attain wholeness is the complete—his existence acquires a meaning. His feeling of merger with the larger body is really a step forward toward this end. Herzog's affirmation leads him to the first step in his purification. Through his self understanding, he attains a mystical level of peace. As Bellow aptly remarks:

> I think a good deal of Herzog can be explained simply by the implicit assumption that existence quite apart from any of our judgments, has value that existence is worthful.... Any Bildunsroman and Herzog is to use that heavy German term, a Bildunsroman concludes with the step. The first real step. Any man who has rid himself of superfluous ideas in order to take that first step has done something significant. (p. 77)

By making his protagonist to take his first real step, Bellow makes him to learn to live with reality without sacrificing heart the vital part. Only contact and engagement can keep the law of the heart alive. Only brotherhood can ennoble human feelings. Herzog has finally learnt that only dialogue can render meaning to one's life—not monologue. He can now cherish the joy offered by life. He is in his right mind again. He has come to terms with his questioning soul. It is suggested that he will work again and it will be a new beginning.

Reference

Bellow, Saul, *Herzog* (New York, 1965). Subsequent references in parentheses are to this edition.

8

Mr. Sammler's Planet

Mr. Sammler's Planet (1970) restricts itself to the vision of its eponymous hero, a sepluagenarian possessed of a good right eye, dark-bright, full of observation, and left eye that distinguishes only light and shade. Sammler is in many ways an outsider. A Polish Jew born in Cracow of Anglophile parents, he fell in love with England as a school boy, and two decades in London as a correspondent for the Warsaw press has left him with idioms more suited to Oxbridge than to his Polish heritage. He has the face of a British Museum reader, and the sensibility as well. Indeed, he is a man reborn not just once, as an ersatz Englishman but several times and in several different ways. Arrested by the Nazis during a visit to Poland to liquidate the estate of his father-in-law, he was beaten and left for dead in a mass grave with his wife dead beside him. After killing a German soldier while hiding in the countryside, he was concealed by partisans in a tomb, from which he emerged once again into life, although into a sense of only half life. His days in Manhattan in the late 1960s constitute still another rebirth into half life, for he perceives a frenzy of play acting in the heightened passions of the period. 'Just look', he thinks at this imitative anarchy of the streets these Chinese revolutionary tunics, these babes in unisex toy land, these surrealist war chiefs, western stagecoach drives Ph.Ds. in philosophy, some of them. They seem to him not authentic revolutionaries but 'Hollywood extras', concerned with 'acting mythic' and casting themselves into chaos, hoping to adhere to higher consciousness, to be washed up on the shores of truth. As fascinated he is carefully fair minded, he watches from the sidelines.

But watching the drama of life in New York draws Sammler against his will into dealings with its cast of characters—with their projects, their shameful little secrets and their needs. A young entrepreneur named Lionel Feffer who haunts the fringes of academe strikes up an acquaintance and inveigles Sammler to deliver the Columbia lecture that result in a challenge to his sexual adequacy. A cousin named Walter Bruch inflicts upon the unwilling old man a strangely varied discourse: reminiscences of Buchenwals, Chaplinesque imitations of Hitler and his Nazi henchmen, and lurid accounts of masturbating behind his briefcase while ogling the arms of Peurto Rican women. Dismayed by the ignorance of university students that his niece pays to read him classic texts in the history of civilization, Sammler finds it necessary to step out of his carapace and 'to teach them the subject, explain the terms, do elymologies for them as though they were twelve years old.'

Even one eyed observation behind dark glasses is treacherously involving for Mr. Sammler Detecting a gorgeously dressed black pickpocket operating regularly on his bus route, Sammler finds his observation observed, and in a surrealistic development the pickpocket follows Sammler, confronts him in the dark lobby of his apartment building, and without saying a word displays his penis in what is generally thought an atavistic gesture of intimidation. Learning of the episode, Feffer later photographs the pickpocket in action in the hope of publishing a journalistic expose, and Sammler is forced to call for aid when he sees the two men battling in the streets for possession of Feffer's camera. To his horror, his son-in-law Eisen overreacts to his insistent call and having been an agent of the danger to Feffer, Sammler finds himself the agent of a terrible beating Eisen administers to the pickpocket. The sequence of events suggests that involvements escalate dangerously on the planet of Mr. Sammler drawing old men into situations from which age and infirmity might be thought to exempt them.

Another sequence of events is set in motion by Sammler's reluctance to disabuse his daughter Shula of her conviction that he is writing a memoir about H.G. Wells, whom he knew for some years in Bloomsbury and whose conversation he listened to attentively. When a Hindu biographysicist named Govinda Lal visits Columbia University to lecture on moon travel, he makes a glancing allusion to Wells's idea about interplanetary colonization, and Shula promptly steals his manuscript to aid her father in writing the nonexistent memoir that has become her obsession. Horrified when the theft is brought to his attention, Sammler arranges for the manuscript into the wilds of Westchester—involves him, too, in a thirty three page, conversation with Dr. Lal that is the novel's intellectual centerpiece.

In a tangential chain of events, Sammler is also drawn into family squabbles that surround the death bed of his nephew, Dr. Elya Gruner, a gynecologist who has helped Sammler financially for many years. In recognition of his father's affection for Sammler, Wallace Gruner asks Sammler to learn from his father the location of money he believes the doctor to have concealed in his Westchester home. A daughter named Angela also asks Sammler to intercede with her father, lest Gruner should cut her out of his will in impatience with her dissotude life. To both requests Sammler turns a deaf ear but when Wallace starts dismantling the plumbing of the Westchester house in an effort to find the cache of money, Sammler cannot ignore the water swirling across the floors of the house and when Angela protests she cannot bring herself to make things up with her father, Sammler cannot refrain from suggesting that a woman who performs fellatio on perfect strangers can marshal the poise to make peace with her father. The novel ends with Dr. Gruner's death and Sammler being admitted to the hospital morgue, where he prays for Gruner's soul.

Mr. Arthur Sammler, the seventy plus intellectual humanist hero of Bellow is an European Jew. He is the only direct survivor of the Holocaust in the fictional world of Bellow. While the Holocaust witnessed the ruin of his family, he himself had been buried by a Nazi execution squad and dug up his friend before he died. Sammler had regained his life by killing face to face a German soldier. Presently in New York city, he tries to behave human and to keep his humanity intact. But Sammler's voice of authority appears to be impotent in a city caught by sexual madness. Although he was born in a past era, he is a modern man caught in a cruel and senseless mass civilization and is falling apart. While Bellow's earlier heroes had come to terms with reality and embraced humanity through meaningful participation in it after a temporary state of alienation, Sammler in a sense is far from alienation.

Despite Sammler's being turned into a detached observer of man and society, the novel is a work of affirmation. Sammler still believes in the potentialities of the human self and of action. The richness of life is never far from his consciousness. Sammler's faith in community and in the importance of moral action is asserted after having been tested in the Holocaust. Sammler has not only survived, but he has continued to live in the post-Holocaust world. But what ails him is that the dehumanized forces of an urban civilization have made ethical accomplishment almost impossible. Sammler knows that it is a world that offers no dignity to the individual self. To assert one's freedom, one has to accept limitations. Unbridled exercise of freedom can result only in chaos and disorder. It cannot bring order and meaning sought for by each of Bellow's heroes. It is only in behaving exactly human that the individual self can discover its true identity. In spite of this, continuing his life in the face of death Sammler behaves in accordance with moral laws and continues his longing for true human dignity.

Sammler tries to behave humanely for which values are indispensable because "A desire for virtue was no accident". Like earlier Bellow's heroes, he feels out of place amongst a crazy species. Distinguished with the sexual madness of the youths, Sammler cannot cope with the naked realities of a modern city existence in New York. He feels suffocation in the quivering riotous, lurid New York, a gas city:

> New York was getting worse than Naples or Salonika. It was like an Asian, an African town from this standpoint.

> The opulent section of the city were not immune. You opened a jewelled door into degradation...straight into the state of nature, the barbarous world of colour erupting from beneath. It might be barbarous on either side of the jewelled door. Sexually for example. The thing evidently...consisted in obtaining the privileges, and the free ways of barbarism, under the protection of civilization property rights, refined technological organizations and so on. (*MSP*, p. 8)

The biggest city on earth has been overpopulated and crime ridden. It is a waste where individual life appears to be disorganized and where only dehumanized forces have come to rule. Individual self seems to be lost in this decayed environment:

> How very heavy human life was here in forms of bourgeois solidity. Attempted permanence was sad.... Did one have a right to private expectations, being like those bubbles in the flusk...what formerly was believed, trusted, was now bitterly circled in black irony.... People justifying idleness, silliness, shallowness, distemper, lust-turning former respectability inside out. (p. 9)

Through Sammler's dissatisfaction Bellow implies that no human life is worthy of its meaning without values. Civilization must stick to and rest on values. Bellow equates erosion of values with death:

> New York makes one think about the collapse of civilization about Sodom and Gomorrah, the end of the world.... Many people already bank on it. And I don't know whether human kind is really all the worse. (p. 244)

Because Sammler believes in the worth of human life, and cannot believe that it was the end, his heart is sad to notice such degradation: "But it is in the air now that things are falling apart, and I am affected by it" (p. 244). Bellow does not hide his irony that such a degenerated human condition exists in America: "Advertised throughout the universe as the most desirable, most exemplary of all nations" (p. 10).

Technological advancement does not count human values and it has its negative effects on the finer qualities of human beings.

Although Sammler claims for himself to be a distanced personality and despite his dissatisfaction, he cannot escape the direct experience of the 'sexual militancy' of the present day youth. While returning one day by bus to his apartment, he discovers a pickpocket committing his crime. Sammler behaves as a 'fool' in reporting the crime to the police, who remain indifferent. Sensing certain troubles, the Negro pickpocket threatens Sammler with same idea of sexual potency that has caught the young generation by a frenzy:

> There the man held Sammler against the wall with his forearm. The umbrella fell to the floor.... The pick-pocket unbuttoned himself. Sammler heard the Zipper descend.... He was directed silently to look downward. The Blackman has opened his fly and taken out his penis. It was displayed to Sammler with great oval testicles, a large tan—and purple uncircumcised thing a tube, a snake; metallic hairs bristled at the thick base and the tip our led beyond the supporting, demonstrating hand, suggesting the fleshy nobility of an elephant's trunk.... Over the forearm and fist that held him, Sammler was required to gaze at this organ. No compulsion would have been necessary. He would in any case have looked. (p. 42)

Sammler is at once astonished as well as repelled by the 'session' initiated by the pickpocket. On the conscious level Sammler admires him for his mastery and dexterity. In short, the black has nobility that appeals to Sammler. But as an intellectual, he is frightened by the irrational phallic power of the mad irrationality in this civilization. To be sure, the pickpocket by demonstrating his sexual potency comes to symbolize what has gone wrong with modern civilization. This is his predicament as an intellectual, Bellow suggests.

Disgusted as he is with the present sexual madness, incidentally he has to experience another incident which brings the idea to the surface that power at present lies in sex. Anyone devoid of sexual potency is powerless. But this incident not merely symbolizes sex for power, but for life itself with sexual potency. Lionel Feffer, one of his exreaders and himself a busy seducer finds time to invite him to deliver a lecture at Columbia on "The British Scene in the Thirties". Before Sammler can move halfway his lecture, the young audience grows impatient and one of them shouts that Sammler is telling shit:

> Why do you listen to this effete old shit? What he has got to tell you? His balls are dry. He's dead. He can't come. (p. 36)

Sammler becomes aware of the vast indiscipline that rules the present youth. If he symbolized order and authority, he finds that most of the young people seemed to be against him. He cannot exert his authority, because he has lost his sexual power. It is not values but sexual potency—indiscriminatory use and exhibition of it—that matters most to the American youth. What saves Sammler is his feeling of somewhat separated from the rest of his species. The intellectual humanist within Sammler is pained to see the outcome of the Enlightenment:

> A full bill of demand and complaint was therefore presented by each individual. Non-negotiable. Recognizing no scarcity of supply in any human department. Enlightenment? Marvelous. But out of hand. Wasn't it? (p. 29)

Sammler knows that the only contact with the eternal is through freedom. But he is at odds with these mad people and finds himself helpless for not being able to do anything for their cure. These people, Sammler is convinced, are after wrong notion of freedom. He is fomented by what he believes is a lunatic civilization, worshipping sex and madness. He asks:

> Who had raised the diaper flag? What had made shit a sacrament? What literary and psychological movement was that? (p. 39)

Sammler therefore finds that the post Holocaust world is not an easy place to lead a moral life. Virtue here not only goes unrewarded, but seems powerless to alter the shape of society, to make it humane. Despite his feeling of powerlessness to effect any correctness, Sammler expands much energy in his attempts to restore values, to get a handle on the situation. Sammler is too conscious of his role as a guardian of society and culture:

> He was a man who had come back. He had rejoined life. He was near to others. But in some essential way he was also companionless. He was old. He lacked physical force. He knew what to do but know power to execute it. (p. 232)

One can posit here that it is not merely the Sammler and the Herzogs who feel companionless, but any human being who stands for values and tries to defend humanity finds himself alone and to be powerless in the present debased state of affairs. That real freedom accompanies with it a sense of responsibility is doomed under the pressures of the city, the dehumanization and the anonymity. If he feels companionless and a crisis of his identity as a true human being amid the mad crowd of New York, he is also a rebel in that he acts as the guardian of the society and culture. He wants to restore order and meaning out of the chaos and senselessness that have come to grasp of the soul of the individuals around him. His endeavour is to show the way of how should a good man live. Sammler knows that man has to live on this earth accepting his limitations and exploring his possibilities. Herein lies his hope of redemption. It is true that the modern existence has turned itself into a sort of business in the present mechanized environment. Too much intellection on man's life has only made the situation worse:

> Life, when it was like this, all question and answer from the top of intellect to the very bottom, was really a state of singular dirty misery. When it was all question and answer had no charm. Life when it had no charm was entirely question and answer. The thing worked both ways. Also, the questions were bad. Also, the answers were horrible. (p. 225)

Sammler like earlier Bellow's hero is not prepared to accept the version of life offered by intellectuals. Despite he acknowledges the fact that society at present has come to crush the individual self, he cannot agree to view that human potentialities have been lost for ever. Sammler would not agree that human life has lost its meaning in the present civilization. He has his firm conviction that the self has still immense possibilities even in the face of a dreaming reality:

> By a convergence of all minds and all movements the conviction transmitted by this crowd seemed to be that reality was a terrible thing, and that the final truth about mankind was overwhelming and crushing. (pp. 224-25)

Sammler rejects this vulgar, cowardly conclusion with all his heart.

True, Sammler has observed and experienced himself the debased human condition in a technological America. But it is his faith in human life based on values that has prevented him from being taken away by idea of a bright future on Moon, put forward by the Indian scientist Dr. Govinda Lal. Dr. Lal is a Punjabi who witnessed the terrible fighting between Hindus and Muslims in the Indian partition in the late forties. Lal advocates leaving this world with the aid of technology. Despite their ideological schism, the two men understand and like each other at once, for both have witnessed suffering. But the main similarity between them is that both seek the answers to the problem of maintaining cultured life in a mad world. Bellow presents a point of contrast here. Sammler has a mystical bent of mind and holds life to be a mastery beyond comprehension, whereas Dr. Lal comes up with the idea of starting life anew on moon with the help of technology. It is to be kept in mind here that Dr. Lal comes from India, the land of the mystics and Sammler is from Europe, of the rationalists. Lal retains no hope of restoring meaningful life on this earth. He rather hopes that the wholeness of the individual self would be fulfilled on moon:

> ...colonies on the moon would reduce the fever and swelling here, and the passion for boundlessness and wholeness might be found more material appeasement. Human kind, drunk with terror, calm itself, sober up. (p. 145)

Sammler is sceptical of a bright future on moon without affecting any moral change. He refuses to abandon his planet—this earth. He is aware that at least America, if not the whole world, was staggering if not breaking up and also that:

> Everything was being done to make earth—a glorious planet—intolerable by an unconscious collaboration of all souls spreading madness and poison. (p. 109)

But he feels that this is not a reason enough to leave this planet. Here Sammler sees the problem from not merely America but global perspective. Desiring a chance of heart, he wonders, whether man's conquest of space would affect any such change without any change in his psyche:

> As for the world, was it really about to change? Why? How? By the fact of moving into space away from earth? There would be changes of heart? There would be new conduct? Why because we were tired of the old conduct? That was not reason enough. (p. 228)

In fact, Sammler disapproves the idea of moving to moon from the very beginning. It is the love for life that makes him convinced that if it were a rational matter then it would be rational to have justice on this planet first. Sammler has made it clear that his planet is not mere American, but the earth itself. There are hints that despite the injustice and inhumanity offered to him and to his family, Sammler has not grown to be a misanthropist. Rather, the reason has added a newer awareness in him—has taught him to live his life for others with a feeling of affinity with God:

> When you know what pain is, you agree that not to have been born is better. But being born one respects the powers of creation, one obeys the will of God with whatever inner reservations truth impose.... The pain of duty makes. The creature upright, and this uprightness is no negligible thing. (p. 117)

Sammler has thus been able to cultivate pain and transform it into a joy of living. If the lesson of suffering urges him to continue life, it also makes him feel oneness with other suffering people. The experience of pain has made him aware of his existence and also, of the mystery of human life created by God. The sense of the presence of God leads him in the way of love, in an incomprehensible way that does enable him to feel for and finally join humanity. This is transformation of a Bellow's hero.

Sammler rejects the idea of fleeing to moon and wants to continue life on this planet. But by now, one should be convinced that he does not want to continue life in its present debased condition surrounding every sensitive individual. Sammler makes his mission explicit that restoration of norms and faith is necessary to make life meaningful and thus renders order and beauty to it:

> The best and purest human beings, from the beginning of time, have understood that life is sacred. To defy the old understanding is not bonality. There was a conspiracy against the sacredness of life. Bonality is the adopted disguise of a very powerful will to abolish conscience. In such a project trivial. Only human life is trivial. (p. 17)

Like earlier humanist Bellow's heroes, Sammler too launches his battle against the conspiracy against the sacredness of life. Because human is no trivial but beauty and greatness, there must be some order, so that each individual self can realize its potentialities. The spiritual recovery of mankind must be affected by removing the present debased human condition:

> Hearts that get no real wage, souls that find no nourishment. Falsehoods, unlimited. Desire, unlimited. Possibility, unlimited. Impossible demands upon complex realities unlimited. Revival in childish and vulgar form of ancient religious ideas, mysteries, utterly unconscious of course—astonishing. Orphism. Mithriam, Manichacanism, Gnesticism. (p. 183)

Sharing with Bellow Sammler rightly feels that a state when man does not accept limitations, the individual self will be far away from salvation:

> The idea of the uniqueness of the soul. An excellent idea. A true idea. But in these forms? In these poor forms? Dear God! With hair, with cloths, with drugs and cosmetics with gentalia, with round trips. Through evil, monstrosity, and orgy, with even God approached through okcenities. (p. 184)

At no point, Sammler's search for values has come to denote that he is not prepared to accept changes of time. He justly acknowledges that the idea of self has undergone changes with the passing of time. Accepting the undeniable impact of a mass civilization on the individual self, Sammler throws a question that Bellow has relentlessly been attempting to explore in depth:

> This too great demand upon human consciousness and human capacities has overtaxed human endurance. I am not speaking only of moral demand, but also of the demand upon the imagination to produce a human figure of adequate stature. What is the true stature of a human being? (p. 186)

He answers the question for himself and comes up with an idea of an individual at present, while hinting at the demand stature of an individual self in the present mechanized civilization:

> The self may think it wears a gay new ornament, delightfully pained, but from outside we see that it is a mistake. Or again, the personality of which the owner is so proud is from the wool-worth store, cheap tin or plastic from the five-and-dime of souls. Seeing it is in this way, a man may feel that being human is hardly worth the trouble. Where is the desirable self that one might be?.... That depends.... It is right that we should dislike contrived individuality, bad pastiche, bonality and the rest. It is repulsive. But individualism is of no interest whatever if it does not extend truth. (p. 188)

Sammler makes explicit his belief that the true notion of individuality must extend truth, must conceived and breath values. But to attain such a state it is necessary that a man has really a desire to exist as a human being. Sammler combats the idea of non-being:

> ...there is a peculiar longing for non-being. As long as there is no ethical life and everything is poured so barbarously and recklessly into personal gesture this must be endured. (p. 188)

Again and again what Sammler insists on is the restoration of good human qualities. While asserting his own humanity, he wants to set a moral dimension on life. For this, Sammler argues, that order must be recovered.

To affect such a recovery that would render to each individual self, its true dignity, Sammler comes to express his faith that a change of heart and faith in God is necessary. It will enable each individual to be aware of true love against all the present vulgarities life's great architect-love seems to be powerless in the face of all present bonalities. Sammler views that it is love and not the present vulgarities which may show the self its way of redemption. God as the spirit of spirits permeates this love in every human soul:

> ...God is the spirit of all spirits. The fruit of the spirit is love, joy and peace. (p. 203)

By this Bellow has hinted that there are still human qualities—there are still Man with capital M. In the character of Elya Gruner, one of the adorable creations ever created by Bellow, he shows that still there are men capable of fostering the message of love.

Indeed in Gruner, Bellow epitomizes love and touch of true human heart. Gruner behaves exactly human. An exceptional character in Bellow, Gruner is a rich man who has made money from his medical practice and from real estate. Noticeably enough, he has remained generous in contrast to other rich people who turn out to be mean. He is a kind man and Sammler rightly tells that it is because of the likes of Gruner that one has to give a second thought before leaving this planet to some others. He makes it amply clear that it is because of the touch of the human heart of persons like Gruner that human life has not fallen into abyss. Sammler praises this ability of love and genuineness of heart in Gruner, while being frank of his own limitations:

> I don't care for the way Elya courted everyone, tried to make contract with people, winning their hearts, engaging their interest, getting personal even with waitresses, lab-technicians, manicurists. It was always so easy for him to say 'I love you'. (p. 242)

In fact, Bellow as a novelist has been persistent in his appeal to develop such capacity:

> ...for delight and wonder—our sense of pity and pain, to the latent failing of fellowship with all creation—and to the subtle 'but invincible conviction of solidarity that knits together the loneliness of innumerable hearts... which binds together all humanity—the dead to the living and the living to the unborn. (p. 79)

In relation to Elya, Bellow thus voices quoting Joseph Conrad one of his major convictions. As Sammler makes it clear that although everybody is superficially born human, to be human is not a natural gift at all:

> It's not a natural gift at all, only the capacity is natural. (p. 244)

It by now becomes evident that with a keen desire to restore order and values to make human life meaningful in its true dignity of this planet of earth itself. Sammler states in clear terms that it is love and the touch of genuine hearts which enables one to complete assignment of one's life meaningfully. This means that only with the feelings of love in his heart a man is able to embrace the whole world feeling oneness with humanity. In communion with others, a man can discover his true dignity of being a human:

> We have our assignments, feeling outgoingness, expressiveness, kindness heart—all these fine human things which by a peculiar turn of opinion strikes people now as shady activities. Openness and candour about vices seem far easier. Anyway, there is Elya's assignment. That's what's in his good face. That's why he has such a

> human look. He's made something of himself. He hasn't done badly.... (p. 243)

Elya Gruner acted exactly human, not more and not less. Gruner represents the essential virtues of the ordinary life according to custom, tradition and duty. Accepting limit actions, Gruner knew what it means to be human:

> He didn't like surgery...he dreaded those three and four hour operations. But he performed them. He did what he disliked. He had an unsure loyalty to certain pure states. He knew there had been good men before him, that there were good men to come, and he wanted to be one of them.... I don't come out nearly so well myself.... But Elya...accomplished something good. Brought himself through... I've learnt much from him. (p. 243)

What Sammler has learnt from Gruner, one is inclined to believe, Bellow intends to learn by every individual. This is Bellow's message to humanity voiced through his protagonist:

> I am not sure that this is the worst of all times. I always hated people who declared that it was the end. What did they know about the end? From personal experience, from the grave if I may say so, I knew something about it.... Anybody may feel the truth. But suppose it to be true—true and not a mood, not ignorance or destructive pleasure, or the doomed desired by people who have botched everything. Suppose it to be so. There is still such a thing as a man—or there was. There are still human qualities. Our weak species fought its fear, our crazy species, fought its criminality. We are an animal of genius. (pp. 244-45)

Reference

Bellow, Saul, *Mr. Sammler's Plannet* (Harmondsworth, 1977). Subsequent references in parentheses are to this edition.

9

Humboldt's Gift

Humboldt's Gift (1975) is narrated over a period of five years by Charlie Citrine, a writer in his fifth decades of life, a native of Chicago, a Knight of Frances's Legion of Honor, and the winner of Pulitzer Prizes for his historical melodrama *Von Trenck* and for a book on Wilson and Tumulty. Although plagued by financial suits brought by his former wife, Denise, and be sotted with the charms of his current lover, Renata Koffritz, Charlie is distracted by the news that the late poet Von Humboldt Fleisher has left him something in his will. Indeed the novel is largely about distractedness. In a dense, multilined flow of narrative, Charlie juggles the story of his relationship with Humboldt and awareness of life within and about him. His intellectual stagnation after the failure of his most recent book disturbs him particularly, the developing failure of his collaboration with a man named Pierre Thaxter on a projected journal of ideas called *The Ark* worries him, and judges, attorneys, and IRS plague him financially. At the same time, Renata's obvious wish to be married and her occasional dalliance with a mortician named Flonzaley keeps him emotionally anxious. Von Humboldt Fleisher looms in Charlie's mind as an obligato to all these awareness, commanding attention, troubling memory and challenging everything that he is.

In *Humboldt's Gift* Bellow portrays the trauma of two literary artists—Von Humboldt Fleisher and Charles Citrine. Both have been the victims of dehumanized world which seems to run through money and power leading man to live in a world of false values. While trying to strike a note of balance between art and power in order to elevate "the human enterprise, so grand infinitely varied" (*HG*, p. 29), Humboldt failed his enterprise and died a terrible death in disgrace. Poets are of no use in a technological America, "symbolism, his school was used up" (p. 161). Business oriented America has no need for cosmic poetry. Technology has replaced poetry in America. Not the poet but technology now performs service to mankind. What led Humboldt to failure Bellow seems to imply is that he failed to integrate his poetic visions with his ideas and his ideas with the actual ways of living. By trying to live a marvellous Humboldt he ignored certain basic facts of life and suffered. In the main, he failed to acquire the only symbol of accomplishment of American culture—money. With full of schemes for making money, he failed to wed it to art. He could not be a rich American poet. His failure in financial terms gnawed him. Citrine's consciousness at present is frequently haunted by Humboldt, who has been a memory and feels a sort of bond with him tied by the chord of love. In fact, presenting two worlds of love and beauty on one hand and of wealth and money power on the other, Bellow once again vindicates that love of fellow humans is what makes a man humane and imagination must overcome intellect. As Humboldt says to Citrine:

> ...remember we are not natural beings but supernatural beings. (p. 347)

Humboldt being dead, it is the tribulations of Citrine which are main concerns of the novel. In depicting the predicament of Citrine as a product of contemporary conditions Bellow once again, and this time, more forcefully and in clear terms, weighs the human against the non-human. Citrine is put into a world where money and technology threaten to nullify the power of art an imagination altogether. The setting is Bellow's favourite city Chicago to which Citrine too feels a sense of belonging. But Chicago has become inhuman and torturous. His beloved Chicago, to which Citrine returns against the desire of his domineering wife, Denise, has become a city of murder and crime, power and money forces which destroy the inner calmness of all sensitive souls. Reality has become indeed terrible for Charlie Citrine who is dragged to the court by his wife and stripped off of a last hope of consolation from his second mistress Renata who leaves her mother and child with him to marry her former lover. Added to this Citrine's present involvement with a racketeer, Rinaldo Cantabile who deprived him of all calmness by creating chaos and disorder in his inner self.

The inevitable results of all this distracting forces have been that, like Herzog's his intellectual pursuits have come to standstill. Citrine is alienated—he feels a sense of displacement. Setting himself against these dehumanized forces, Citrine comes to represent the loss of inner life and hope of a modern man. What Bellow shows through Citrine is that the private existence of the self is distracted by the destructive rationalism of a technological civilization. Putting Citrine against these forces and by charting out the path for spiritual survival in a post modern society, it is Bellow's purpose to show the possibility of moral transformation, which enables one to come to terms with life and reality. By this one can attain the true meaning of one's individuality. A man can attain his true identity only when if his self can survive and Bellow shows that this is still possible against all modern trivialities. Citrine's rediscovery of the self—his victory over these distorting forces of a mass civilization shows the victory of the human against the dehumanized elements given birth to such an environment.

Citrine finds his life in great disorder in a mass society where "Few people seemed to be consummating anything good these days". It is a lifeless bureaucratic society where private life has been brought under tremendous pressure of public sphere. Here the government too wants to measure the value of human soul in financial terms. It is a world ruled by gangsterism and everyone seems to be caught by 'money fever' in Chicago "a cultureless city pervaded nevertheless by Mind" (p. 69). The mass society has identified money with freedom. The mystic power now belongs to money:

> When you get money you go through a metamorphosis. And you have to contend with terrible powers inside and

> outside. There's almost nothing personal in success. Success is always money's success. (p. 375)

Like Joseph and Wilhelm, Citrine is "still at the primer level in my understanding of money" (p. 159), and forced by the environment, he is involved with a racketeer Rinaldo Cantabile in a poker game. The underworld prince Cantabile comes to represent the urban ugliness that threatens to crush the finer and beautiful elements of human life.

After the poker game, Cantabile chases Citrine with his demand of money. But to heighten the intensity of the relation between the two, Bellow makes Cantabile not to be content with the satisfaction of his monetary demand Cantabile chases Citrine further. The relationship between the two reminds one of the relationships between Leventhal and Allbee in *The Victim*. Like them, Citrine and Cantabile are alternately fascinated and repelled by each other. Citrine even believes that a natural connection existed between us. One of the main intentions of Bellow in developing the relation between the two is to show the grovelling of art under money. By its enchanting power, money has trespassed into the intellectual world. Cantabile wants to purchase talent with money. His wife teaches at Radcliffe and has been working for her Ph.D. on none other than Von Humboldt Feisher. He demands help and data from Citrine in order to complete her project. In the long scene depicting the conversation between Citrine and Cantabile, Bellow lays bar—the present condition of artist intellectuals in money ruled America where art has become a commodity on sale. Hinting at a kind of love-hate relationship between Citrine and Cantabile, Bellow presents a culturally degenerated civilization where even the underworld monster longs for a higher life:

> Cantabile had invested much boldness and ingenuinity in me and now he seemed to feel that we must never part. Also he wanted me to draw him upward to lead him to higher things. (p. 174)

In consonance with the tune of time, Cantabile therefore proposes a mutual deal. He has a desire to do good to Citrine: "I can put you into a good things" (p. 174). A good businessman, Cantabile remains true to his promise which he fulfils by helping Citrine to have a contract relating to the copywright of a screen play *Coldofreddo* co-authored by him and Humboldt. Assisting him in making the deal regarding his claim to the genuine authorship of the story, Cantabile does not forget to claim his own commission. Citrine thus feels the Romance of business which his rich elder brother was always talking of.

To be sure then money has become an all pervading force in an urban industrialized society, which not merely attempts to corrupt the individual self, but at its annihilation altogether. "Ten grand to-day will get you fifteen by Thursday. That's fifteen percent in three days. Fifteen percent" (p. 265) as Cantabile reveals America thus has been a harsh trial to the human spirit. Citrine is aware of the meagre modern existence, of identity by conditioning forces of society:

> Gertrude Stein used to distinguish between a person who is an entity and one who has an 'identity'. A significant man is an entity. Identity is what they give you socially. You little dog recognizes you and therefore you have an identity. An entity, by contrast, an impersonal power, was be a frightening thing. (p. 311)

By possessing his mere identity, the individual self has become a dwarf in the face of a giant society. Man has lost the power of true soul under the terrible attack of conditioning forces: "The great feelings and thoughts are gone" (p. 294). As a result, man has lost his inner strength and beauty:

> But this calls for unusual strength of soul. The more so since society claims more and more and more of your inner self and infects you with its restlessness. It trains you in distraction, colonizes consciousness as fast as consciousness advances. (p. 306)

Such distractions have deprived man of his inner spirit. The outcome is a deep feeling of tedium that leaves no man free. It is against these forces. Citrine seems to argue that man has to struggle to keep intact the beauty and strength of his soul. It is not possible:

> The true poise, that of a contemplation or imagination, sits right on the border of sleep and dreaming... determined to resist its material interests and hoping for redemption by art. I fell into a deep snooze that lasted for years and decades.... America is an over whelming phenomenon, of course. But that is no excuse.... Luckily I'm still alive. (p. 306)

What is evident, therefore, is that if money tries to corrupt the individual self, the overall social environment comes to assist in this and would not allow an individual to have an inner life. It is content to offer a mere identity to an individual, not allowing him to be an entity. It is this scene of loss of the self in a mechanized world that leads Citrine to write his master project on 'Boredom', for Chicago is the ideal place:

> My subject...was boredom. Chicago was the ideal place in which to write my master essay 'Boredom'. In raw Chicago you could examine the human spirit under industrialism. If someone to arise with a new vision of Faith, Love and Hope, he would not want to understand to whom he was offering it—he would have to understand the kind of deep suffering we call boredom. (p. 250)

Like earlier Bellow's heroes, the intellectual Citrine with his humanist outlook, 'having pursued a higher purpose and trying to do some good' sincerely wants to prevent the leprosy of souls. What he wants, in fact, is to live with his true soul and not allow the pretender soul to rule over it. He also refuses to allow a world hostile to potency to shape his values or mould his tastes. Citrine laments the diminution of the private self by the intrusion of a huge destructive public sphere. The public sphere, he arouses, has made values recoil from human life and thus resisting its redemption:

> The greatest things, things most necessary for life have recoiled and retreated. People are actually dying of this losing all personal life, and the inner being of millions, many millions, is missing. One can understand that in many parts of the world there is no hope for it because of famine or politics dictatorships but here in the free

> world what excuse have we. Under pressure of public crisis the private sphere is being surrendered. I admit this private sphere has become so repulsive that we are glad to get away from it. But we accept the disgrace ascribed to it and people have filled their lives with so called public questions. (p. 250)

Obviously then, in such a society there will be more 'It' than 'We'. Viewed in a global perspective, Citrine thus comes to profess one of Bellow's primary concerns. It will be recalled that through his earlier heroes, Bellow has repeatedly and forcefully affirmed his faith in the potentialities of the self to be realized within imposed limitations. He has also ascertained that to attain true human dignity, one must behave exactly human viewed from this angle, one can discern a note of maturity in Citrine and also noticed in Mr. Sammler. Citrine has come to profess his faith not merely in the possibilities of the individual self in relation to history and time, but his mind has been touched by a still higher idea—the immortality of soul in the continuous chain of life cycle:

> ...I do not believe my birth began my first existence. Not Humboldt's. Nor anyone's. On the esthetic grounds...I cannot accept the view of death taken by most of us...on the esthetic grounds therefore I am obliged to deny that so extraordinary a thing as a human soul can be wiped out for ever. (p. 141)

Citrine at the same time makes it clear that to have his communion with the true soul a man must have freedom. Here he voices another of Bellow's recurrent ideas that to gain freedom, one must accept both sides of the case:

> We are free on earth because of cloudiness, because of error, because of marvelous limitation, and as much because of beauty as of blindness and evil. These always go with the blessing of freedom. (p. 141)

Bellow has always viewed the motion of freedom not in a narrower scale but in a larger perspective. Bellow earlier made it explicit that every individual, guided by some mystic power, feels a bond of unity, incomprehensive to his consciousness, with other beings of the universe. It is his own inner resources of a Bellow's hero that more often than not offer suddenly a clue to the true meaning of his own being and then only can feel oneness with humanity. It is the real freedom for a Bellow's hero. Citrine too believed in the power of thinking as a source of freedom. Citrine does manifest another of Bellow's faith that each individual being a tiny part of the larger cosmic order is bound to all other beings in some incomprehensible way. Everything taking place within a man's psyche, therefore, has a wider significance:

> ...I was by inclination the sort of person who needed micro cosmic—macrocosmic ideas or the belief that everything that takes place in man has world significance. Such a belief warmed the environment for me, and brought out the sweet glossy leaves, the hanging oranges of the groves where the unpolluted self was virginal and gratefully communed with its Maker, and soon. It was possible that this was the only way for me to be my own true self. (p. 257)

In agreement with Citrine, one can perhaps argue here that it is the invincible faith of Citrine in the indestructibility of the omniscient soul invariably related to other beings in the greater cosmic order that has urged him to retain his true soul. Because of this faith he has survived his struggle against the distracting and distorting forces of modern society. Bellow perhaps hints that it is the strength of 'the true soul' as against that of 'the pretender' one which he helps man to retain true human dignity against all oddities of life. As Citrine's friend Thaxter unfolds:

> ...your character is a very peculiar one but there is a certain—I don't know what to call it—dignity that you do have. If you say soul and I say psyche you have your reason for it, probably. You probably do have a soul. Charles. And it's pretty startling fact about anyone. (p. 271)

The main point, Bellow stresses, is that because everyone has a soul, its sanctity must be preserved to make one's life meaningful. To be human is to attain true dignity. Life is beauty and greatness only when one's soul is not polluted. Like

Herzog, Citrine with his altruistic vision, makes it clear that it is in the values and not in a corrupt mass society in the present debased condition that a man can have his true stature and dignity. Such a state is the only truth which enables a man to have communion with divinity that permeates each human soul with love and wisdom. Only sticking to his true soul enables an individual to exist as a human in his struggle against the dehumanized forces because it is these forces which not only want to pollute but to eat up the 'true soul'. Citrine views the problem in a global perspective:

> And O! We poor souls, all of us unstable ignorant, perturbed, so unrested.... Failing in the night to make contact with the merciful, regenerative angles who were there to strengthen us with their warmth and their love and wisdom. Ah, poor hearts that we were, how badly we were all doing and how I longed to make changes or amends or corrections. Something. (p. 267)

Despite the wreckage caused to his emotional life by his wife Denise and his mistress Renata and despite the fact that even a 'soldier of culture' like him has to come to terms with underworld figures Citrine desires to survive against all void. Having asserted his belief in the immortality of human soul he stresses on its purity. Thus Bellow once again vindicates his hero's love for life and his aspiration for true human stature. It is what Citrine exactly desires. He wants to exist as human and 'to do something' so that salvation of each individual soul is made possible. He wants to restore order to render each individual life beauty:

> And if we will not awaken, if the Spiritual Soul cannot be sought to participate in the work of Angels, we will be sunk. (p. 294)

Like Sammler, Citrine comes to express his faith in God as 'the spirit of spirits'. Angels bestow love on mankind, who have corrupted it. But for salvation to be made possible, its genuineness must be restored:

> Among the things they wish to make us see the concealed dignity of the human beings. They show man he can cross by means of thought the abyss that

> separates him from spirit.... Their aims must be realized in earthly humanity, itself. Already the brotherly love they put into and has been corrupted into sexual monstrosity. What are we doing with each other in the sack? Love is being disgracefully prevented. Then, too, the Angels send us radiant freshness and we by our own sleeping, make it all dull. (p. 294)

Citrine reveals in clear terms that without restoration of order and values, salvation of mankind is not possible. For this one can depend on the power of imagination that directly springs from human soul. It is still capable of struggle with corrupt forces of the world:

> The world was interesting, really interesting. The world has money, science, war, politics, anxiety, sickness, perplexity. It had all the voltage. Once you have picked up the high voltage wire and were someone, a known name, you couldn't release yourself from the electric current...interest follows power. Where are the poet's power and interest? They originate in dream states. These come because the poet is what he is himself, because a voice sounds in his soul which has a power equal to the power of societies, states and regimes you don't make yourself interesting through madness, eccentricity or anything of the sort but because you have the power to conceal the world's distraction, activity, noise and become fit to hear the essence of things. (p. 312)

Once again Bellow pinpoints his conviction that the individual self is still possessed of its potentialities. It can still survive the conspiracy of the powerful conditioning forces of the world. What is necessary is that one must be capable to hear 'the essence of things' that originates with one's imagination itself. Such faith in the power of imagination makes Bellow's stance clear that art is still something worth holding to in this age of mass technology. Citrine cannot believe that imagination must be asked to give up its own full and free connection with universe. He says in clear terms that the scientific world view cannot explain every human nature:

> ...the individual has no way to prove out what's in his heart—I mean the love, the hungering for the external world, the swelling excitement over beauty for which there are no acceptable terms of knowledge. True knowledge is supposed to be monopoly of scientific world view. But human beings have all sorts of knowledge. They don't have to apply for the right to love the world. (p. 314)

More scientific formulations cannot explain complex human nature. It cannot reach and touch the human heart. It cannot teach man in the art of love leading to universal brotherhood. It is important before the basic human qualities like love, sympathy, kindness and brotherhood. Science is unable to teach man to behave as human in a world where money has pushed art back to the pit and dollar have come the soul's husband. To live a meaningful life in an age like this one must learn to understand life. For this, Citrine seems to hint; one must look inward, and delve deep. The illumination that teaches a man to behave as a true human being must come from within. For this, however, a man must have his striving. He must retain his faith in such a power and stick to his striving amid the distracting forces of a technological world:

> The strangeness of life, the more you resisted it harder it bore down on you. The more the mind opposed the sense of strangeness, the more distortions it produced.... Moreover I was convinced that there was nothing in the material world to account for the more delicate desires and human perceptions of human beings. (p. 439)

The persistent endeavour of Citrine has been to revive faith in the power and worth of art and imagination that springs in the inner recesses of a man's soul. He wants to revive culture in a culturally degenerated materialistic America. Citrine feels this task has a greater implication than merely fulfiling his own destiny. The restoration of culture is a business with him 'on behalf of the entire human race'. Because the present civilization has made the idea of individual freedom a paradoxical one in that the soul of a civilized and rational individual appearing to be free, is really confined and negligible one. The state being as it is the only hope lies in the salvation of the soul:

> But to assume, however queerly, the immortality of the soul, to be free from the weight of death that everybody carries upon the heart, presents, like the relief from any obsession, a terrific opportunity. (p. 442)

It becomes evident from the final analysis that though his protagonist, Bellow demonstrates the possibility of the survival of the self and art in modern industrialized America. Citrine knows that the individual ego will return to dust, but believes, nevertheless, that human soul is beyond the reach of all these trivialities of reality. It is eternal. Against the distractions created by a modern machine civilization, Citrine through his life and deeds, shows that it is still possible to maintain a meaningful private existence and by which one can still have a decent approach to life. To put the matter in a different way, it is the values and not the hodge-podge of a material outlook which renders meaning to one's life and thus making the salvation of the soul possible. Beyond the material and the historical Citrine endeavours to see 'the essence of things'. He manifests that to be truly human, inner culture of a man must not be stagnated. Citrine does recognize and accept the fact that the real life is a relation between here and there. It is in this way that he comes to terms with death.

Through his protagonist Bellow expresses his vision of the struggle of the human self to survive. Bellow never tries in showing that for such a mission to make success, one needs to learn the art of love. Like other Bellow's heroes, Citrine has his faith in the power of love. The final scene of the novel depicting the reburial of Humboldt is in fact an act of love. But, as David C. Dougherty says, this reburial, this performance of love is also a celebration of life. If the act signifies Citrine's joining humanity, it also prepares him for a direct enjoyment of and confrontation with life. He has learnt to come to terms with reality:

> But then, how did one get out? One didn't, didn't! You stayed, you stayed. (p. 487)

Reference

Bellow, Saul, *Humboldt's Gift* (Harmondsworth, 1984). Subsequent references in parentheses are to this edition.

10

The Dean's December

The Dean's December[1] (1982) is Bellow's tale of two cities Chicago and Bucharest. The protagonist, Albert Corde, is a newspaper man who has become a professor of journalism and subsequently dean of students in an unnamed Chicago college. As dean, he has embroiled himself in controversy by writing a series of articles indicting Chicago for its racism, its clubhouse politics, and its lack of what he calls 'moral initiative'. He has also pressed for the conviction of a black man who murdered one of the college's white students, and he has endeared himself thereby neither to the college provost nor to young liberals on the campus—among them, his nephew. In short, the dean is too morally passionate for Chicago. He has jeopardized his professional standing as both journalist and college official by his impulse to take absolute moral readings.

The dean is geographically, if not mentally, distanced from the Chicago fray when he and his wife Minna spend the month of December in Bucharest visiting her dying mother, the distinguished psychiatrist Valeria Raresh. From the outset of their stay, they find that a Rumanian official obstructs their visits to the dying woman, apparently because of Valeria's history of disdain for the Socialist government. Thirty years earlier she had fallen into disfavour as minister of health, officially exonerated years later, she had declined to rejoin the party. The government officials respect Minna's international standing as an astrophysicist, but she had defected from Rumania twenty years earlier while studying in the west, and they are not disposed to overlook Valeria's behaviour for her sake. Indeed, because she did not formally renounce Rumanian citizenship when she became a citizen of the United States, she is arguably subject to Rumanian authority, a situation that worries Corde. Incautious conversation must never be indulged in her mother's wiretapped apartment, he warns, and he is anxious that they leave as soon as possible after Valeria's death on Christmas eve.

A childhood friend of Corde named Dewey Spangler happens to be in Bhucharest when Valeria dies, and Corde confides in him, imprudently so, because Spangler is an international journalist who fancies himself a Walter Lippmann. Upon the dean's return to America he is embarrassed to find that he has given Spangler an interview and is the subject of one of his columns. Insidiously, the column mimics the dean's articles about Chicago in one tone and style, and with pseudo-analytical eloquence Spangler concludes that Corde possesses 'earnestness too great for his capacities'. So damning is the indictment and so dismissive Spangler's suggestion that Corde went into shock when he glimpsed the world outside academe Corde feels his professional credibility destroyed, at least in moral matters. He resigns his deanship immediately, intending to write further articles but no longer attracted to controversy. The novel ends with him accompanying Minna to the Mount Palomar.

In fact, it is not so much a tale or novel as it is the record of the ideas and opinions which float through the mind of Albert Corde, as he observes the people and the surroundings around him and the events happening to him. John Updike is not incorrect when he says that *The Dean's December* is essentially a "non-fiction book inside the novel".[2] Michiko Kakutanic tells us how after his trip to Israel in 1975 Bellow had an urge to write about "great public matters": "The winning of the Nobel Prize in 1976 no doubt provided some of that necessary confidence, and he made plans to write a non-fiction book about Chicago. After making hundreds to abandon that approach and write a novel".[3]

Albert Corde, the protagonist, is a good observer of things, but others too observe him, and what they observe is none too flattering at least not so to Albert Corde:

> Valeria had never made Corde feel that she objected to the marriage...she did study him. Yes, but without apparent prejudice. Really she was fair-minded. Although he hadn't much liked being under observation, he conceded that it wasn't unreasonable. "But Christ do I need a parole officer"? Of course he was uncomfortable, and when he was uncomfortable he grew more silent, speaking only in a brief rumble what was most distressing about being watched was that it made him see himself—a dis-faced man, long in the mouth. You could hardly blame him for being sensitive to close scrutiny. (*DD*, p. 12)

That is Albert speaking about his mother-in-law. The experience can well be viewed under the aspect of Sartre's formulation in respect of the encounter between the 'being-for-itself' and 'being-for-others'. To Albert Corde, Valeria is the 'other'; Albert Corde, the being-for-itself, experiences, acute self consciousness in respect of this 'other'. The passage quoted above amply demonstrates that he is extremely self-conscious. He does not shape himself in accordance with the image others have of him.

Even Minna, his wife, thinks that Albert is a muddled man; "She was wondering quietly about him. What sort of man is Albert—what is his quality"? (p. 14) It is not that the marriage is on the rocks as is in some of other novels of Bellow. But Albert Corde is certainly an island unto himself. The sister of Albert, Elfrida says of him:

> She was perhaps as sorry for her brother as he was for cousin Max. She believed he was a very strange man. His hangs-up were not like other peoples—identifiable neuroses, alcoholism, bragging. Nothing normal. He had his own most original, incomprehensible way of screwing things up. (p. 98)

It is relevant to mention Albert Corde's relationship with his nephew:

> Given encouragement, Corde would have liked being kindly candid, affectionate, but Mason gave no encouragement, wasn't buying any kindly candor, and Corde was careful with him, never uncled him, never lectured. (p. 32)

Corde is a well-read man. His talks and his articles carry evidence of his reading of Plato and Aristotle, reading of Dante, Shakespeare and Milton. He is well aware of the different traditions of thought, the different forms of society. But Corde's notations are not very incisive. In fact, he tends to make easy formulations and categories. He tends to punctuate his writings with platitudes to focus attention on the surface details:

> It was an instinct with Corde may be it was a weakness —always to fix attention on certain particulars, in every situation to grasp the details...with him, exclusively mental acts seldom occurred. He was temperamentally an image man. (pp. 16-17)

These suggest that Corde is not sure of himself and is beset with certain contradictions and confusion. For the most part he remains a passive figure, not so much a participant in the action as a witness to the action. Perhaps that is the reason why the critics have labelled the book as non-fiction in nature Albert Corde and his wife, Minna visits Bucharest to see her dying mother. What strikes him about Bucharest is that like Hamlet's Denmark it is a city under surveillance; every citizen is under observation so to say. The institutions show rigid regiment of heart, free and frank exchange of views is not to be permitted. Corde is a virtual prisoner there. He shuts himself up in his wife's room and keeps looking out the window. While in Bucharest, he has some unpleasant encounters too. But again these things are not so important. What is important is Corde's perception of the culture of Bucharest. Bellow uses this perception as a foil to Corde's experience of Chicago.

Bellow himself has talked freely and frankly about the culture of Chicago. In his interview with Roudane, Bellow makes the following observations:

> I add that Chicagoans have for the most part escaped contamination by pseudo culture. I say "for the most part" because television and cultural journalism do great of Chicago. Still the "ethnic neighbourhoods" resist with admirable stubbornness you ask why I live here, and what I give in reply is a minisermon against the vanity of seeking "the great good place" the ideal situation. There is no such place.[4]

In the same interview Bellow goes on to say:

> Environments matter, but they do not determine being. Being towers over them. To cover oneself with labels or shut oneself up in pigeon holes is also one of our own deliberate choices. There are times when the genius of our species, for mysterious ends of its own, needs to create something like a nation of Chicagos. A surrender to desolation is not, however, acceptable to spirited people. One must rather try to decipher the necessarily obscure message concealed within the appearances. Perhaps this is what you meant by 'existentialist'.[5]

The Dean writes articles recording his impressions of the culture of Chicago. He writes about violence and abuse to be found there. He writes about the rising crime graph and about corruption. Albert Corde's fraternity does not take kindly to these articles. Even some of his relatives turn against him. The dean himself is not too happy, neither with himself for speaking the truth, nor with those who are critical of him because he has spoken the truth. The fact is that Albert Corde's response to Chicago is itself marginal. He has not yet reached the level of consciousness which will permit him a gestalt view of Chicago or of Bucharest. Consider, for example, Albert Corde's response to the death of a White students in a bar brawl. Two Black students are accused of causing the death. As a Dean, Corde has to involve himself in the murder trial. He knows that the death was accidental, but he hopes that the verdict will go against the two Black students. The episode shows the limitations from which Albert Corde's consciousness suffers.

In his articles Albert Corde always talks of the loss of ancient virtues in our times. The following passage should make it clear:

> A tender liberal society has to find soft ways to institutionlise harshness and smooth it over compatibly with progress, buoyancy, so that with us when people are merciless, when they kill us, we explain that it's because they have disadvantaged, or have lead poisoning, or come from a backward section of the country, need psychological treatment. (p. 305)

Albert Corde has glimpses of the wholeness of the past. His problem is that he himself fails to reach it. His transcendence, what Sartre would call his 'leap of faith', comes when he gets the courage to throw away his tenure and decides to go to Mount Palomer. The focus in *The Dean's December* is mainly on the manifestations of social disorder. As in other novels, here too the protagonist's development is on by now the familiar Sartrerian lines. Albert Corde also transcends his various acts of bad faith, and moves towards self-definition, his 'essence'. *The Dean's December* is, in some ways, a failed novel. Bellow's aesthetic weight is more on the manifestations of social disorder than on the predicament of his protagonist. It is true that Bellow rounds it off well. Albert Corde is allowed a vision of wholeness and integration but that is more predicated on him than enacted through action.

For sometime Bellow had been working on a long non-fiction book about Chicago, which, he came to realize, could only be given its due in fictional treatment. Chicago, he told an interviewer, was "a subject for some kind of poetry, not a factual account", or "the very language you have to use as a journalist works against the true material". Another case of public life is drowning out of private life. Bellow's protagonist, Albert Corde, a former journalist and professor of journalism turned dean of students at a Chicago university also knows that "nothing true—really true—could be said in the papers". Inspiration came when Bellow fused the Chicago book with one about Bucharest a tale of two cities, as was *Humboldt's Gift*. It is as if Bellow of late needs to rub two stones together to make the sparks fly. While this strategy was successful enough in the earlier novel, there is some question as to whether it is in *The Dean's December*. Bellow told the interviewer that he had written that the novel materialized as a pleasant surprise: "I wrote it in a year and a half and had no idea it was coming". But he told another interviewer that he had written the novel "under great pressure—a book club deadline" and that he was sick when he finished.

The book does show some signs of strain. Without the usual galvanizing act (e.g., the pickpocket's exposure or the Columbia scene of *Mr. Sammler's Planet*) or galvanizing character (e.g., Henderson), the new novel is one in which Bellow's discursiveness overwhelms his sense of fable. In its casual reflectiveness, it can sometimes read like notes: "That would be a good question. What did Corde represent?" (p. 131) Occasionally the pain it describes seems gratuitous, as in the kidney dialysis description, where the author seems to be rubbing our noses in metaphysical waste. More importantly, the juxtaposition of the east and the west remains linear, undramatized with the result that Bellow's vivid portrait gallery remains too often just that Bellow's transitions are mechanical: "Now to move to Valeria and the life support machines" (p. 105): "Abruptly, Bucharest again" (p. 156); "To resume" (p. 158); "And now, with stormier objectivity, himself" (p. 122). In *Mr. Sammler's Planet* the death-bed scene was brief and affecting. Here, within a bureaucratic nightmare, we are given a death-bed scene longer than that in any opera. Valeria's hand stirs by page 127. When, toward the novel, Corde picks up a manila envelope of mail, the present action intensifies. Event is disproportionately retrospective. Citrine did a stretch of recollection lying down, but Corde spends much of his time in cold, hostile Bucharest under the covers as he ruminates about the "rum" in Rumania.

The Dean's December is a tale of two dismal cities. Bucharest is a disaster, an instance of "the penitentiary state". The people who once embraced the Russians and built post-war Rumania are now grovelling under the iron, bureaucratic boot. Yet the "hard nihilism" of the Soviet bloc makes civilized gesture that much more touching. The small female band of intimates in Bucharest is like delicate flowers growing out of stone, the most minimal strumming yet of the axial lines. But from a dramatic point of view they are not worth all the description Bellow lavishes on them. Gigi, for example, is too dull for so much attention. She is not as interesting as the sad communist city itself. In the rendering of urban place, Bellow is superb as ever.

Where Bucharest is full of debilitation and death, Chicago is full of depravity and decadence, the "soft nihilism" of the west. Bucharest is cold, Chicago is hot, and it seems that Bellow is posing his version of Frost's question—will the world end in fire or ice? A certain darkness has fallen on Bellow's Chicago that makes necessary human connection nearly impossible. The qualified buoyancy of Augie March is long gone. Chicago is now the contempt "center of the U.S.A.", and there is nothing quite like "the crying ugliness of the Chicago night" (p. 44). In fact, "Chicago was not Chicago any more" (p. 237) according to Alexander Corde. We know how bad things are when he judges today's Chicago to be worse than New York. Like other Bellow's protagonists, Corde is a reader of Blake, but Blake here means "Cain's city built with murder" (p. 285). Representative in many ways of the ultimate nihilism, Chicago is a "mass of data, terrible, murderous" (p. 266), like "advanced modern consciousness" itself, which, "because its equipment was humanly so meagre, so abstract, was basically murderous" (p. 193). Another value seems headed for oblivion, the value of ordinary possibility, of spirit rising out of the democratic mass.

The novel makes it clear than ever that "Looking for Mr. Green" is one of the central pieces of the Bellow canon, for the radical split between appearance and reality dramatized in the early work—which, as we have seen, gains currency in such later works as *Mr. Sammler's Planet* and *Humboldt's Gift*—is dominant in *The Dean's December*. Some lines in the book might have come from the short story. Corde "would have liked to tell his nephew that men and women were shadows, and shadows within shadows, to one another"

(p. 32). When Corde climbs the stairs to the detoxification centre—again the upward quest in slum setting—he thinks, "If there was another world, this was the time to show itself. The visible one didn't bear looking at" (p. 189). The contemplative Dean attends to his surroundings "As if he had been sent down to mind the outer world, on a mission of observation and notation" (p. 210). His task is "to recover the world that is buried under the debris of false description of non-experience" (p. 243). The Bellow's protagonist is still looking for Mr. Green, though in the novel the obscurity has cultural roots. Still, doxa all but buries episteme. There is no Platonic harmony. The French Huguenot—Irish Corde might better have been named Discorde.

This critic noted with mistrust Charlie Citrine's lucubration about the fallen world of appearances. Corde all but lapses into cynicism "Nobody had a good connection or knew what racket he was in—his real racket", he thinks Corde, "that he might, at last be headed in the right direction" (p. 32). He notes of Valeria that "for her this world of death was ending world of death? He surprised himself when he put it that way" (p. 133). Again Corde eludes the grasp of nihilism, but in a troubling, passive way considering the energy with which the Bellow's protagonist—Herzog, for example—usually assaults it. The line of Shelley about George III that he associates with the unsavoury Detillion—"the old mad blind despised and dying king"—is a psychic refrain indicating a lack of paternal principle, secure morality. When, at the end of the novel, Corde stares into the cold of interstellar space, does he derive any more comfort from the sight than does Stephen Dedalus? Herzog ridiculed Heidegger for falling into the quotidian, but what is Corde's emphasis on the falseness of newsprint, the inauthenticity of the everyday, if not Heidegger's *Verfallenheit*? "Social communication is the doom of every truly felt thought" writes the novelist, but the novelist is Mailer, not Bellow. From this premise, Mailer goes subjective and experimental, writing a more verbal fiction. Bellow deeply opposes this direction loosening one's moral stance, dismissing tradition as only a joke, going further into subjectivity, into the erotic of art—these merely add to the already existing problem. Tied into monologue though he often is, the Bellow's protagonist leaves the way to the objective world open. In *The Dean's December*, he does so almost in spite of himself.

For the citizen hero in Bellow, marginal at best, has come on particularly hard times. With his nostalgia for use, his nose for public issues, his distinction as a political journalist, his perception of communist rot, Corde is this hero more clearly than any other Bellow's surrogate. He is, in fact, doing his Harper's articles on Chicago prisons and hospitals with "the high intension—to prevent the American idea from being pounded into dust altogether". But the rhetoric here is excessively defensive. Rufus Ridpath and Toby Winthrop are two black men who prove that the virtue of the citizen is still possible, even if their lives finally leave Corde with anger or depression.

As he leaves the detoxification centre Corde's talk about high intentions is immediately qualified by the realization that "the facts were covered from our perception", that "the first act of morality" was to find the real in the garbage of unreality and, odd perhaps for a journalist but not a novelist, "represent it anew as art would represent it". Dewey Spangler, the political journalist and Corde's adversary, is right in scoring "poetry" in so far as it is poetic gesture, "but not in so far as Corde was genuinely inspired. In so far as he was inspired he had genuine political significance" (p. 123). His political significance is the exposure of a spiritual failure. Corde, then, sees significance in the occasional inspired or courageous citizen but not in the conventional "rational citizen's courage", since one cannot be "managerial and noble at the same time" (p. 276). His Chicago articles are a testimony to this perception. Even academe, in his grim view, is "dominated by the same consensus and ruled by public opinion" (p. 301). So much for the politics of civility, yet the transformation Corde desires may admit only of pragmatic solution.

Is Corde inspired? Can he be, in his own terms, considering that he is a journalist? Only as a maverick super journalist, perhaps, it is, of course, the novelist who may create inspired art. But there is some question as well as to whether Bellow himself is here inspired art? Indeed, the author is so dismissive of everyday life that one may wonder whether realism can do justice to his contempt. Bucharest and Chicago are all but fantastic in their repressiveness, and Bellow is now playing a humanists' version of endgame. It is now the Bellow's protagonist who abyssifies.

Yet for all his talk about apocalypse, one ought not to suppose that Corde is enamoured of it. He has "no sermons to preach about the death of cities or the collapse of civilization" being "too much of a Chicagoan to feel up to that", that is, in the last analysis retaining somehow enough of the ordinary human stuff. Like Herzog, he rejects playing at apocalypse, considering "this poor man make believe...a dangerous distraction". Corde sees clearly that "this a time of the breaking of nations" and, of course, cities. The "real temptation", however, is not that he will advocate the apocalyptic but that he will "hope that the approach of 'last days' might be liberating, might compel us to reconsider deeply, earnestly". More precariously than ever, the Bellow's protagonist is on the side of civilization. Mistrusting the prophetic, he tries to hang on against all odds to the ethical. "I personally think about virtue and vice", says Corde, courageously square (p. 277). The Bellow's protagonist still looks for individual responsibility, but his task has become rather like that of Diogenes because of recalcitrant social conditions. Corde embodies this responsibility. Though he has paid a price, he still says what he wants. His nervous decency is contemporary.

References

1. Saul Bellow, *The Dean's December* (New York, 1982). Subsequent references in parentheses are to this edition.
2. John Updike, *Hugging the Shore: Essays in Criticism*, p. 256.
3. Michiko Kakutanic, *On His Work and Himself* (ed.), Sukhbir Singh, op. cit., pp. 137-38.
4. Matthew C. Roundane, "Junkyands are as Miraculous as Orange Groves", (ed.) Sukhbir Singh, p. 147.
5. *Ibid.*, p. 148.

11

More Die of Heartbreak

More Die of Heartbreak (1987) tells us about a relationship between two men: thirty-five year old Kenneth Trachtenberg who narrates the story and Benn Crader who is his maternal uncle. Raised in France by American expatriate parents, Kenneth has returned to the American Midwest and taken a position teaching Russian Literature at the same Rustbelt University that employs his uncle. Benn is a world class botanist, a specialist in the anatomy and morphology of plants but Kenneth sees him fondly as one of those old time Kansas banks that any bank robber could knock over. A wider Benn proves especially vulnerable to women. Profoundly distressing to him is the memory of a neighbour named Della Bedell who laid a manic claim to his sexual favours and whom he evaded by arranging a lecture tour in Brazil. In the wake of her death shortly afterward a newspaper reporter asks for a statement about the effects of nuclear radiation and Benn makes the remark that gives the novel its title:

> It's terribly serious, of course, but I think more people die of heartbreak than of radiation.

Kenneth's uncle marriage to Matilda Layamon, daughter of a wealthy gynecologist is really a concern to him. It develops the plan to make Benn a millionaire. Benn has no sympathy with the scheme but he fails to take action against his uncle and departs secretly for the North Pole with an international team of scientists leaving Matilda to have their marriage annulled if she chooses. His escape from Mrs. Bedell is the pattern of his escape from Matilda, as it was the pattern of his escape from Matilda's immediate predecessor, Caroline Bunge whom he abandoned almost at the altar. Who was it, Benn asks his nephew in parting, who described him as 'a phoenix who runs with arsonists'?

As Kenneth counsels his uncle and listens to his problems often in that order, he suffers vaguely analogous difficulties. Treckie Sterling, the mother of his daughter, but not his wife as he frequently reminds us, has moved to Oregon, where she is cohabiting with a burly Ski instructor. In the manner of his uncle's women Treckie's mother subsequently makes a bid to marry Kenneth. 'Not for me, thank you ma'm', Kenneth mutters, but Mrs. Sterling's less-than-sterling proposition inspires him to visit Treckie and his young daughter. On his return to the Midwest, he turns with increasing affection to a former student named Dita, no beauty or socialite but a gentle woman. The novel's imagery of fire and polar ice belongs to Benn's emotional life, not to Kenneth's but Kenneth is to some extent a phoenix like his uncle, and his heart experiences a modest resurrection at the end.

More Die of Heartbreak is about love, or, rather, it is about what has happened to love at the moment in history that is defined by the America of the novel, which Kenneth calls variously the 'post historical age', the 'post human age' and the 'age of desire'. Modern Western Culture has laid such emphasis on materialism that all higher human powers are despised. In the terms of the novel, human need and aspiration have been channelled into the erotic and while the erotic itself has shrunk to an animal appetite, men and women still perceive erotic failure as human failure. But as Kenneth sees it even erotic success is problematic. Erotic love is now mere self-gratification, and as such it is destructive of the self and careless of its object. The poet William Blake (who figures frequently in this novel) wrote of self-centred love in 'The Clod and the Pebble':

> Love seeketh only Self to please
> To bind another to its delight,
> Joys in another's loss of ease,
> And builds a Hell in Heaven's despite.

This is what Matilda Layamon would do to Benn, turning him into a kind of highbrow tourist attraction for her dinner guest, but the novel provides a more chilling image of the way in which self-pleasing 'love abuses another in Benn's account of the parole hearing about the rape of Danae Cusper. After his violent act of self-gratification the rapist used a broken bottle to cut the word 'LOV' into the girl's abdomen. This cynical mutation of love into 'LOV' corresponds to the mystical appearance of a small glacier in each human breast, described to Kenneth by his first Russian teacher, M. Yermelov. The glacier can only be melted by the warmth of human love, which men now resist.

The repression of human need into a simple erotic imperative is destroying us all. Benn's flight to Brazil is precipitated by the attentions of Della Bedell, a lady who lives in his apartment building. Plain, short and fat, she cannot generate desire in another. Benn goes to bed with her almost accidentally, and when later he avoids her she puts notes in his mailbox. "What am I supposed to do with my sexuality"? The situation is farcical, yet it reveals the despair of the erotic failure. While Benn is in Brazil Della dies of a cardiac arrest, for which he blames himself: 'I see her suffocated by swollen longings'. It is this idea that prompts him to respond to a journalist who asks about the radiation level in plants with the statement that provides the novel with its title: 'I think more people die of heartbreak than of radiation'. This is not a remark intended to dismiss or minimize the threat of radiation, but Benn's point appears to be that a preoccupation with material destruction has made us neglect the far more widespread spiritual destruction that results from the disappearance of love. Della's story has its counterpart in that of Dita Schwartz who, also suffering from swollen longings, undergoes the extreme physical pain of a medical treatment that amounts to self-laceration in an effort to make herself erotically desirable for Kenneth.

As Kenneth sees it, this confusion about love and desire arises because the world is suffering from a division of the physical from the spiritual, and he seeks from himself a higher mode of living. As he says,

> You have no reason to exist unless you believe you can make your life a turning point for everybody—for humankind.

This may seem a grandiose view to hold of the significance of one's own existence but in Kenneth's case it is an insistence on an ethical need, for his life to set a pattern that goes against the current of contemporary circumstances. The experience of the novel seems to suggest that it is impossible to live in the world without being communicated by it, unless you can be, like Benn, 'a man capable of living fully in isolation from the life of his time'. Kenneth sees Benn quite seriously as a genius, a man close to becoming a 'Citizen of Eternity', ranks with the likes of Moses, Odysseus, the Prophets, Socrates, Mozart, Pushkin and Blake. Benn's genius lies in his peculiar, even transcendent, ability to see into the lives of plants. It is literally represented in terms of vision: the oddity of Benn's eyes is frequently stressed as Kenneth describes them as being like a figure eight turned on its side, producing a disturbing gaze 'when you felt the power of looking turned on you'. The power of looking, of a vision that goes beyond surfaces, beyond the material, is also indicated metaphorically here, for the titled figure eight is the sign for infinity. Benn's preternatural vision is what Kenneth refers to as his 'magic'; his eyes are receptive, taking in what others do not see, which in itself generates that superiority that makes him a candidate for Eternal Citizenship: 'Man is what he sees'. Kenneth's own ambition is to go beyond Benn, to learn from his uncle's magic to bring to the human world the vision that Benn brings to plant life. This is how he will make his own life a turning point for mankind.

This is all serious stuff, but the novel is, nevertheless, comic, Benn's ability to be in tune with natural harmonies might in this context be defined as 'love', and we should note the consolation he receives from contact with a Christmas tree during his wedding ceremony. He falls into the material world of 'LOV' when he becomes attached to Matilda Layamon, and the comedy arises from his struggles to understand this world and then to free himself from it. Matilda is a woman of high intelligence, though this is exhibited in an interest in literary fascists. Her family lives a lifestyle of opulence and doubtful taste mainly intended to advertise its wealth, and Matilda, with her peculiar exotic and brittle kind of beauty, a 'glittering, nervous, French-Mid-western woman', fits well amongst the furnishing. The ambiguity of the Layamon household is underlined by Dr. Layamon's attitude to both his wealth and his daughter, veering between boasting and virulent criticism. It is also emphasized by the prurient interest of this gynecologist in his daughter's sexual activities. He is one more in Bellow's line of fast-talking confidence tricksters, and the corruption of his values, in comparison to Benn's clear vision or straight gaze, is implied by the distortion of sight indicated by his crooked spectacles: 'Doctor's eyeglasses didn't sit level and his glances, too, were skewed'.

Benn becomes a part of this uncongenial household because, like everyone else, he needs love and thinks it can be found. He convinces himself that he has found it in Matilda by making an almost Platonic assumption that her physical beauty represents an inner beauty. Consequently he ignores his instincts, which send him warning messages about her. These come, comically, through the film psycho, which Benn hates because it gains its effects through sensationalism and emotional manipulation, and, worse still, because he feels himself respond to it. His identification of Matilda's shoulders with those of the mad killer in the film is one of a series of signs that disgust him, but that he nevertheless suppresses. His marriage; then, is a denial of his nature and it is presented in the novel as a fall. The mythic overtones are made quite explicit. At the start of his narrative Kenneth imagines himself making a painting of his uncle in which Benn is pictured in a clearing in a forest partnered with a tree in the 'green seclusion' of what Kenneth calls a 'modern-dress Eden'. The echo of the 'green shade' of Andrew Marvell's poem 'The Garden' is unmistakable; like Marvell's paradise, this one works because it has not been invaded by a woman:

Such was that happy Garden-state
While man there walked without a mate
....
Two paradises 'twere in one,
To live in Paradise alone.

As if trying to hold on to his Eden, Benn embraces the Christmas tree at the moment of his marriage, but he cannot prevent his own fall once he is in the midst of the fallen world of the Layamons, as is indicated by his failure to realize that Mrs. Layamon's azalea, from which he has felt himself deriving comfort, is artificial. This loss of his botanist's vision, of his 'magic', is what precipitates his flight to polar isolation in the hope of learning to regain his paradise.

Although the novel's focus is on the degeneration of erotic love, this is only a part of wider vision of a world altogether fallen, with no sense of the values of any human purpose. 'We've split things in two, dividing the physique from the mind, Kenneth says at one point, and this division is graphically illustrated by a sequence of scenes which focus the masculine gaze on the female sexual parts: at the Japanese strip-tease show; in the Maimonides Hospital, where Dr. Layamon passes Benn off as a doctor to exhibit to him the private parts of old women; and at the hearing for the Cusper rape case. In each case sex has been turned into theatre to emphasize the separation between object and viewer; this exhibition is, to use Kenneth's word, 'literal' and, as he says, 'To be seen literally dries out one's humanity'. The spectator of such literal exhibitions may be mystified or aroused, but he does not feel anything about the object that he abuses with his gaze. Benn is disturbed by all of these experiences, but most deeply so by the last, because it is here, in this arena of public and political showbiz, that he is forced to recognize that everything is as cynically debased as 'LOV': Crime, Punishment, Justice, Authority, were satirized in this hearing Plus Patience. Plus truth.

In the middle of this mockery of values Benn confronts his uncle Vilitzer, though his intention is not quite to go long with the Layamon's scheme to exert money from the old man.

Vilitzer is a veteran political fixer who has amassed enormous wealth through corrupt dealings; many years ago he cheated Benn and his sister over a land deal from which he himself made a vast profit. In spite of this, Benn retains great affection for Vilitzer, who is lit by the nostalgic glow of Benn's memory of his childhood. Vilitzer responds to such feelings only with contempt, however, resisting even his son Fishl's desperate attempts to elicit a sign of love from him. The supreme realist and crooked fighter, who knows himself to be surrounded by crooks, his creed is that 'Where money is concerned, the operational word is merciless' or, as Kenneth glosses this 'Kinship is bullshit' and he is absolutely resistant to doing the right thing by his nephew. Now little more than a shell of a man, 'as light as an empty plastic egg carton, his heart taken over by a machine, Vilitzer is the novel's grimmest satirical picture of the dehumanizing effect of money. As such, he is appropriately associated with construction of the Electronic Tower, a monument to power and money that throws a sinister shadow across the landscape of the novel.

The Electronic Tower works as a complex symbol, and it gains part of its effect from the way in which characters respond to it. Vilitzer's pride in his association with the Tower relates to its size and its function in generating money. Mrs. Layamon, who can see it from the penthouses window, thinks it is 'an important piece of modern beauty'. The rich and privileged can get from its summit a 'stunning view' of the urban devastation that has been caused in the pursuit of wealth, and in its phallic symbolism it relates to the novels' central concern with sexual self-gratification by implying the erotic attraction of money and power. To Benn, with his deeper vision, the Tower seems to take on a life of its own, at night moving closer to the penthouse building, as if threatening to crush it. He thinks of it as being like the Titanic, with immense potential for destruction. A more complex analysis, that indicates the danger of thinking through metaphor, is presented by Kenneth: 'Skyscrapers, as we all recognize, also express an aspiration towards freedom, arising above. They may be filled with abominable enterprises, but they do transmit an idea of transcendence. Perhaps they mislead us or betray our hopes by an unsound analogy. In his appeal to general agreement Kenneth implicates the reader as a probable victim of misread analogy, and we should turn back to Benn's image of the Tower-as-Titanic, suggesting sinking rather rising.

Part of Benn's life has already been crushed beneath the weight of the Tower, for it is built upon the piece of land where Benn spent his childhood. 'My old life is lying under it', he says, and this is a significant statement because it is in his old life where Benn locates the source of emotional sustenance. He has a rosy vision of his childhood, and he continually reconstructs it in memory as a time of all-encompassing love and kindness. This is why he generates no resentment for Vilitzer, because he cannot detach the man he encounters at the Parole Board hearing from the Vilitzer of his childhood. Kenneth questions the accuracy of what Benn thinks he remembers, suggesting that his recollection of warm family affections is really a fairy tale, but even it is a fairy tale Benn needs it, and he cannot cease loving Vilitzer. The difference between Benn and Vilitzer's son Fishl, who also deeply loves the old man, is that Fishl is pathetic because his love is unrequited, and he needs to be loved in return. Benn can love the old man without needing to have his love requited. But it is his need to love that tricks him into believing that Matilda is a deserving object.

At the end of the novel Benn is defeated. His understanding of love as altruism, as a sympathetic connection with another being, makes it impossible love is only egoistical self-gratification, but he is, to a degree, infected by the Layamon view, and is deeply wounded in the bluntin of his responses to the vegetable world. It is appropriate that he decides to retire to the purifying cold of the North Pole and to the problem of the Arctic lichen which, like the human heart, is largely iced over but which can be revived with a little warmth. This seems a rather pessimistic ending, but as is usual with Bellow's novels, there are complicating factors which veil the novelist's intentions. These are to do first with the narrative voice and second with the relationship between the narrator and Benn.

For all his claim to intellectual clarity, Kenneth is a garrulous an disorderly narrator, the producer of a digressive structure for which he himself has to apologize. He exhibits a smug arrogance that is far from Benn's generosity of spirit, when he contemplates those 'shits' whom he considers to be inferior to himself, 'people of ordinary stunted imaginative powers'. He visits his mother at her mission in East Africa and insists on regaling her with his views on the lost state of the world while failing to note that she is a living example of self-sacrificing love. Only late, and almost reluctantly, does he recognize the true inner beauty latent in Dita Schwartz. He treats his own unworldliness. For examples, he mocks Benn's attempt to express his love in terms of Edgar Allan Poe's poetry as naïve, pointing out the immaturity of Poe's ideas of love, infatuated as he was with a woman locked in a state of permanent childhood, and he only belatedly recognizes that his own attraction to Treckie is to the child-woman in her. In sum, Kenneth admires himself rather more perhaps, than we can admire him.

Still, Kenneth's love for Benn, it has to be said, is very real, as is their mutual dependence. Their relationship is symbolic, each seeming to need the other to complete himself. The seriousness with which they take this has comic aspects: Benn submits his experiences to Kenneth's judgement in order to understand them himself, Kenneth takes notes of their conversations so that he can analyze them. Even Benn's intimate sexual experiences come under this scrutiny, and he is certainly not reticent about describing them, making something of a voyeur out of Kenneth. So close is their attachment that when Benn marries into the Layamon family Kenneth thinks of himself as being carried into the family with his uncle, and when Benn talks about his prospective honeymoon Kenneth feels a twinge of jealousy, as he has been 'cut out'. There are potential homoerotic implications here, of course, which Benn himself is at pains to deny when he rejects theoretical suspicion that men who marry beautiful women may be homosexual. Still, there is a sense that the two men have opted for weakness by allowing their relationship to protect them from the realities of the world, as is indicated by the story from Hoffmann that Kenneth alludes to at the end of the novel, a story which surely does suggest homosexuality. It may be that the love that both of them are seeking already exists between them.

As usual, Bellow obscures his own views by these narrative indirections. It should not be assumed, however, that the narrative indirections and the comic tone are intended to mitigate the pessimism suggested by Benn's retreat from the world. Kenneth's view, illustrated by the story he tells, is that 'historical forces are sending everybody straight to hell'. His conviction that the Western world is in a state of cultural and intellectual crisis was certainly in 1987, a conviction that Bellow himself held.

More Die of Heartbreak is though less acute in its identification of those forces which have hastened 'the declining march of humankind'. Though there is Bellow's familiar attack upon the rampant Philistinism of American rationalistic and scientific culture in all its excessive material forms, this is attributed to 'a huge force that advances, propels...it demands the abolition of such things as love and art' (*MDH*, p. 301); and though the 'historical forces' (p. 68) have their say in this decline, Kenneth, with his background in the Russian mystics, can't resist describing in this huge force in terms of a demonological coup. Apparently angels and demons have been struggling for American souls while they sleep, but angelic love has lost to devilish lust:

> Denied access to the soul, the angels work directly on the sleeping body. In the physical body this angelic love is corrupted into human carnality. Such is the source of all the disturbed sexuality of the present age...planetary demons of electricity were entering us from beneath, coming from the interior of the earth. They filled the spinal fluid with their currents of lust. As the millennium approached its end, this was the true picture of human sexuality. (p. 73)

In *More Die of Heartbreak* Bellow reveals the futility of trying to hold to a humanist ideology in contemporary times. Perhaps this is the sense in which his creation of Kenneth can be viewed for if he in all his feeble personality and tedious speechifying is humanism's defendant, then that hope will remain unregenerate. There is no cure for the spiritual and emotional haemorrhage of our time, and that deaths from heartbreak will go on increasing.

Reference

Bellow, Saul, *More Die of Heartbreak* (New York: William Morrow, 1984). Subsequent references in parentheses are to this edition.

12

A Theft

In 1989 Saul Bellow published two novellas *A Theft* and *The Bellarosa Connection. A Theft* was published under rather odd circumstances Bellow initially offered it for magazine publication, but the editor required that extensive cuts be made. Bellow was unwilling to agree to this, and instead had the book published in paperback form—a very unusual move for a writer of Bellow's stature. The 'theft' of the novella's title does not actually take place until more than mid day through, and the plot built around it is not very substantial and not always coherent.

In *A Theft* Clara Velde is an executive in a publishing company, dealing with matters of fashion. Now in her forties, she is married to her fourth husband, Wilder, by whom she has three daughters. The one real love of her life, however, is the high-flying Washington figure Ithiel Regler, with whom she has had a twenty year affair, and who, in spite of her persuasion that they are the 'human pair' whose children would save the world, has managed over that time to avoid marrying her. Years before, Regler had given her an emerald ring which became for her the sentimental symbol of their love. The ring was once lost, and recovered long afterwards, though Clara did not return the insurance money that she had claimed for it. Now the ring has disappeared again, and she suspects that the Haitian boyfriend of her Austrian Gina Wegman has stolen it. The simple plot tells of her efforts to retrieve the ring, efforts which illuminate and develop her relationship with Regler, Gina and her oldest daughter Lucy.

Clara shares much with the earlier female characters. She is handsome, sexy, with good legs, buys her clothes in the best shops, is full of 'personal force':

> Really, everything about her was conspicuous, not only the size and shape of her head. She must have decided long ago that for the likes of her there could be no cover-up. She couldn't divert energy into disguises. So there she was, a rawboned American woman. She had very good legs—who knows what you would have seen if pioneer women had worn shorter skirts. (*A Theft*, p. 1)

It is possible to see from this passage from the book's opening paragraph what difficulty Bellow had in presenting Clara. The qualification in the second sentence ('she must have decided rather than she decided') implies an unwillingness fully to enter her mind, and the emphasis on the legs reveals a masculine rather than a feminine gaze. It may be that this difficulty of reproducing a feminine consciousness is why so much of the book seems under-developed. The narrative voice that here sees Clara from the outside does sometimes speak from her perspective, but it generally takes an odd, chatty tone that the author seems uncomfortable with. To get round this discomfort he allows Clara to tell much of her own story, to a Chinese-American confidante named Laura Wong. Laura is an essentially passive device, there to listen to Clara. When, near the end of the novella, Clara decides that Laura wants to get Regler for herself, the reader cannot understand it, because Laura is barely allowed to exist as a character:

> She had been married too. Five years an American wife. May be she had even been in love. She never said. You'd never know. (p. 20)

Clara is the most fully realized character in the book, but there is much that we are not told even about her. The product of a small town, God fearing Indiana upbringing, she was educated at Bloomington. Wellesley, Cambridge and Columbia. She worked for *Reuters* for a time, taught classics, and wrote feature articles for foreign newspapers before setting up her own journalistic agency, which she sold to the international publishing company in which she is now an executive. This is quite a career, and her life has involved, as well as her four husbands, numerous lovers and two suicide attempts. The problem is that, although we are told all of this, we see little of it. The world of fashion in which her great abilities have made their mark is hardly described at all, being represented by a suite of offices, a trade briefing on shoulder pads and a show featuring such fashions as puffy knickers and stimulated beaver capes. It is ironic that a woman presented as deep in feeling and thought should have built her reputation out of expensive superficialities.

If the depiction of Clara is insubstantial, that of Ithiel Regler is much more so. Precisely, what he does is never made clear. He is an expert on nuclear strategy, a magnetic television personality who interviews men like Anatoly Dobrynin, a political trouble shooter who has the ear of Henry Kissinger and whose opinions are listened to by the Shah of Iran and the Venezuelan government. He has other large interests, though, helping a Japanese whiskey manufacturer to find a South American market and helping the Italian police to track down terrorists. He only does what he wants to do, however, and when he feels like a break he flies to the Olduvai Gorge to talk to Mr. Leakey, presumably about anthropology. Clara herself has no doubts about his greatness; he is the standard against which all other men are judged, a man who more than any other understands the nature of the times. She thinks:

> Why, Ithiel could be the Gibbon or the Tacitus of the American Empire.... If he wanted, he could do with Nixon, Johnson, Kennedy or Kissinger, with the Shah or de Gaulle, what Keynes had done with the Allies at Versailles. (pp. 55-56)

The improbability of all this does not seem to have escaped Bellow, as the name Ithiel Regler implies.

The problem is to show the quality of such a world class thinker. Bellow had attempted something of the sort with Herzog, Mr. Sammler and Benn Crader. But Regler comes out with ideas like this:

> Neither the Russians nor the Americans can manage the world. Not capable of organizing the future. (p. 56)

And Clara is so impressed by it that she thinks of setting up a fund so that Regler can publish his thoughts. Later, when she is trying to find Gina, who has left home after the theft of the ring, she goes to Ithiel for advice and he suggests to hire a private investigator. Her response is to say to him,

> I can see why General Haig and such people call on you to analyze the Iranians or the Russians. (p. 78)

This response might have been mock-naïve, for Clara "recognized the comic appeal of being the openmouthed rube" (p. 15). But there is no indication here that she does not mean her praise seriously, and the effect is of preposterous inflation.

The relationship between these two, at least from Clara's point of view, is symbolized by the ring. The ring comes to signify not just the love that she shares with Regler, but 'love' on a more general scale. When she loses it, the effect on her feelings is profound, though it hardly seems to worry Regler at all. The loss also affects her relationship with Gina, for whom she has conceived a maternal affection. She sees Gina as an innocent who must be protected from the potentially crushing energies of New York. The trust that has developed between them is violated by the theft of the ring by Gina's Haitian boyfriend, and the fact that it was removed from her bedroom, her inner sanctum, seems to Clara to augment her sense of having violated. The theft lets in the terrible predatory forces of Gogmagogsville, forces that deny love. Consequently, the effort that Gina makes to retrieve the ring becomes a sign of hope for Clara.

Because we see so little of Gina, because her character is so lightly sketched, we do not see why Clara has become so fond of her. The important revelatory function she performs at the end of the story is, consequently, difficult to accept. Clara meets her at the Westbury Hotel to discuss the circumstances of the return of the ring. She discovers that this restoration involved an act of enterprise and maturity by her daughter Lucy. Lucy is a clumsy, persecuted girl whose vulnerability has contributed much to Clara's fears for the future, but Gina shows how much of Clara's strength Lucy has in her. She also points Clara towards a new self-understanding:

> With all the disorder I can't see how you keep track. You do, though. I believe you pretty well know who you are. (p. 108)

The novella ends with a burst of cathartic emotion:

> The main source of tears came open. She found a handkerchief and held it to her face in her ringed hand, striding in an awkward hurry. She might have been treading water in New York harbor—it felt that way, more a sea than a pavement, and for all the effort and the motions that she made, she wasn't getting anywhere, she was still in the same place. (p. 109)

This scene of weeping and drowning is reminiscent of the ending of *Seize the Day*, but whereas the source of Tommy Wilhelm's tears was pity for himself and for mankind, Clara's emotion is affirmative:

> I do seem to have an idea who it is that's at the middle of me. There may not be more than one in a xillion, more's the pity, that do have. And my own child possibly one of those. (p. 109)

A Theft implies much more than it says. We are told of a culture in decline, but the distressed American cityscape that Bellow created so vividly in earlier novels is never shown to us. Instead, the horrors of Gogmagogsville are embodied in the Haitian thief Frederic, who is treated by the narrative with no little contempt—we are a long way from the 'noble' black criminal of *Mr. Sammler's Planet*. The threat to civilization becomes, rather, the threat of Harlem to Park Avenue, and it is difficult to see the pampered fashion consultant with her suite of offices and her livery service as the representative of anything that really matters. Indeed, Clara hardly has the right to resent Frederic's theft of the ring, since she was guilty of a theft of equivalent magnitude when she failed to return the insurance money. The larger meanings attached to the ring, about the need for love in the world, simply to not show themselves with any clarity.

A Theft was intended to be a sort of humanist's fairy tale of Mahattan. Written in what Bellow called 'a sort of holiday mood', there is in it a real sense of happy ending for Clara, whose 'one and only subject' is, according to Ithiel Regler, 'love and happiness' (p. 16). But *A Theft* still contains, Bellow's darling themes: the pressure, the outrage, the determination to have us respond to the reality of such human depletions as Allbee refers us to, are now transmuted into the resignation of irony. The decline of human standards remains Bellow's concern, but anxiety has turned into a wry acceptance, and indignation to the acknowledgement of unstoppable decay:

> Unless heaven itself were to decree that Gogmagogsville had gone far enough, and checked the decline time to lower the boom, send in the Atlantic to wash it away. Not a possibility you could count on. (p. 65)

Reference

Bellow, Saul, *A Theft* (Harmondsworth: Penguin Books, 1989). Subsequent references in parentheses are to this edition.

13

The Bellarosa Connection

With *The Bellarosa Connection* (1989), his second novella, Bellow returned to more characteristics preoccupations: the fate of Jewish people, the future of America, the uses of memory, the value of a life. The 'connection' of the title refers to an organization supposedly operated by the Broadway showman Billy Rose to smuggle Jews out of wartime Italy. One of those he aided was Harry Fonstein, who escaped via Cuba to America, and built a successful business. Driven by a desire to thank his benefactor in person Fonstein spent some years trying to arrange a meeting with Rose, but was always rebuffed, and finally gave up. Sorella, the wife of Harry Fonstein, however, believed that that part of Fonstein's life could never be completed unless he met Rose. Near the end of the fifties she arranged a visit to Jerusalem, knowing that Rose was going there to donate a sculpture garden. Armed with a dossier documenting Rose's shady business and sexual affairs, she confronted him in the King David Hotel, hoping to force him to receive Fonstein. What she found, however, was a contemptible, sleazy figure who had no interest in the lives of those he had aided, and in disgust she left him alone.

This history is recounted to us in the immediate present by a narrator who remains unnamed throughout, though we learn much about him. Born in New Jersey of a Russian Jewish family, he turned his extraordinary powers of memory into a business and built a fortune as founder of the Movemosyne Institute, in which he trained others in the use of memory. He married a woman of old Anglo-Saxon Protestant stock and now, in his seventies, widowed and retired, he lives alone in a great Philadelphia mansion. His life intersected twice with that of the Fonsteins. He first met them forty years earlier, when Harry, the nephew of his stepmother, had just arrived from Cuba. He did not see them again for more than ten years, and then he met them by chance in the lobby of the King David Hotel. This encounter in Jerusalem was the last time he saw them, and the history he gives us derives entirely from these two periods, since the only subsequent contact he had with them was a telephone call from Harry to discuss the education of their son Gilbert, a prodigy in mathematics. At the time of his narrative, however, his interest in the Fonsteins has been revived by a request for help in locating them. His attempts to find them necessitate contacting long-neglected acquaintances, and he finally discovers that died in a road accident six months earlier as they were driving to Atlantic city to aid their son who had got into trouble through gambling.

The main interest in the story derives from the way in which the narrator reconstitutes its incidents through an act of memory, and begins to see a new significance in them: that the Fonsteins, who had long seemed interesting but marginal to him, might have contributed something important to his experience, and that the meaning of the Fonsteins' lives has much to do with the meaning of his own. His narration has a dual perspective, because his accurate memory allows him to recall events from the past exactly as he had originally perceived them, while he is now able to see the inadequacy of that perception, and gropes for a better understanding. Fundamental to this reconstruction is a question raised by Sorella when she tries to explain Rose's behaviour:

> The Jews could survive everything that Europe threw at them I mean the lucky remnant. But now comes the next rest—America. Can they hold their ground, or will the U.S.A. be too much for them? (*BC*, p. 2)

Rose's actions in the story remain something of a puzzle. The real life of Billy Rose was a song—writer and impresario, a night-club owner, a producer of Broad way spectacles of immense vulgarity. He was, that is, associated with the kind of escapist vision of life represented in the novella by Broadway, Hollywood and Las Vegas. Thus the fictional scheme for rescuing Jews from Fascist Europe is directly associated with such fantasy: 'He must've seen Leolee Howard in *The Scarlet Pimpernel*, Ch-1, the narrator suggests, and even the romantic sound of the conversion of Rose's misheard name to 'Bellarosa' holds something of this. Although his actions were prompted by deep feelings of Jewishness, he was not capable of understanding the experience of the European Jews. Sorella presents a truer perspective when she says of the crippled adolescent Fonstein struggling through Italy. 'He couldn't vault over walls like Douglas Fairbanks' Ch-1. Rose's theatrical constructions are a means of evading reality, like the 'Hollywood style' extravaganza he made out of the American Jews' statement against the War against the Jews.

And yet the story of Billy Rose is a great American success story: the poor Jew with cunning and enterprise who knew that in America you can sell anything and who made it big by selling escape. But the kind of escape from reality that he had been selling to the American masses made it impossible for him to understands the reality of the escape that he had made possible for Fonstein. This is what Sorela is referring to when she asks whether the U.S.A. will be too much for the Jews: will it cut them off from an understanding of the special experience of their race? When Sorella confronts Rose and demands that she remembers her husband. Rose asks 'Remember, forget—what's the difference to me?' But Sorella knows that Fonstein's experience was a Jewish experience, 'a part of the destruction of the Jews', and not it to remember it is to deny. When the narrator meets the Fonsteins in Jerusalem he is aware that Harry is still the man who has the contrast between Rose and Fonstein lies part of the answer to Sorella's question.

What America does to the Jew, the novella implies, is to make him forget what it means to be a Jew, to make him forget the suffering that has been the Jewish fate. This theme is explored not so much through the contrast between Fonstein and Rose but through the contrast between Fonstein and the narrator makes when he reconstructs the Fonsteins' story that he is closer to Rose than to Fonstein:

> I was a Jew of an entirely different breed. And therefore (yes, go on, you can't avoid it now) closer to Billy Rose and his rescue operation, the personal underground inspired by *The Scarlet Pimpernal* the Hollywood of Leslie Howard who acted the Pimpernal.... You pay a price for being a child of the New World.

The price he has to pay, communicated to him through a dream, is the discovery that he has never really understood the kind of merciless brutality that is the Jewish experience, such as emblematically represented in the figure of the old mad man in Jerusalem who sets him off on his search for the Fonsteins, 'abused out of his head by persecution, loss, death, and brutal history'.

The story implies that this failure of the Americanized Jews arises from a conscious act of the will, and it is here that the narrator's concern with memory becomes important. Billy Rose's refusal to acknowledge Fonstein is a denial of a part of his own history, and the narrator himself is guilty of a similar denial. His worldly success has its foundation on his own discovery of the commercial potential of memory. This made him a fortune and allowed him to marry a Wasp lady and become a Philadelphian; it also estranged him from his father and his cultural origins, represented by his upbringing in New Jersey: 'Whenever possible I omitted New Jersey', he says, meaning that by an act of will, a denial of memory, he effaced his Jewish roots. His secession from his own history is reflected in his present isolation in his Wasp mansion, but its seeds were there in the past, at the time of his first encounters with Fonstein. Fonstein's sufferings gave him a weight and seriousness that the dilettantish narrator lacked; the latter's self-conscious cleverness is nicely caught in his own description of the contrast. 'Surviving Fonstein, with all the furies of Europe at his back, made me book bad'. The callow wit of the statement manages to acknowledge Fonstein's suffering without in any way understanding it.

The character who does understand Fonstein's suffering is his wife Sorella, the moral centre of the story. Sorella is an extraordinary creation, the comic treatment of her extreme fatness in no way undermines the dignity and seriousness of what she represents. Indeed, the comic treatment is necessary, for it is through transcending the rejection and humiliation that her immensity brought upon her in the past that Sorella was able to achieve imaginative identification with Fonstein's experience and an awareness of the crucial importance of maintaining its memory. Her climatic recognition that Billy Rose is not fit to associate with her husband is in one sense a triumph, a demonstration of her own superiority, but it is also an admission of her defeat by American spiritual vacuity. As a defeat it was prefigured by the narrator, who in response to her attempts to make him think about the Holocaust refused her challenge:

> I didn't want to think of the history and psychology of these abominations, death chambers and furnaces.

It is followed by a rather more terribly ironic defeat.

The Fonstein's son Gilbert is a mathematical prodigy for whom Sorella has great hopes. Summing up, her confrontation with Rose she says 'from start to finish it was a one-hundred-percent American event, of our own generation. It will be different for our children.' But it is not different for Gilbert, who finds a way of selling his abilities, and uses his mathematical genius for developing systems to win at gambling. On a literal level this destroy his parents, for they are killed in a car crash while on their way to Atlantic city to extricate him from trouble that he has got into through his gambling. On a metaphorical level the destruction is greater, for at the end of the novella we are told that he has little interest in being a Jew, and that he is in Las Vegas, 'the heart of the American entertainment industry', operating a gambling system that involves memorizing cards. His career, that is, recapitulates the careers of Billy Rose and the narrator himself, combines show-biz with memory, and implies the inevitability of the corruption of the Americanized Jew.

The ending of *The Bellarosa Connection*, like all Bellow's endings, allows for conflicting responses. This led some reviewers to claim that the ending, does not tie things together, or that it is a conclusion in which nothing is concluded. But perhaps something may be concluded. The final sentence has the narrator recording everything he can remember about the Bellarosa connection 'with a Mnemosyne'. The whole novella, that is, is presented as an act of memory. What does this mean? 'Memory is life', the novella keeps saying, but also 'memory is a curse', Billy Rose sees only the second of these truths, so he refuses to remember. The narrator, more sophisticated in the ways of memory, must find more complex ways to deal with the curse. In a sense, he reverses the position: life is memory; or, perhaps more accurately, a life is a memorial reconstruction. In recording everything he can remember of the Bellarosa connection, in reconstructing the Fonstein's life, he appears to be trying to reconstruct his own and to incorporate his real experience in it. Fonstein's suffering is a part of Jewish history and it must be recognized. This is what Sorella's life means, for it has been dedicated to bringing about that recognition. The narrator's growing apprehension of Sorella's ethical significance, his need of the heroic feminine sensibility, along with his recognition of his failure to understand the Jewish experience of brutality, open up the possibility of a healing awareness. In telling the story he is also learning from it and relocating himself inside Jewish history. Having long desired isolation, he finally finds himself 'with an acute need for conversation'.

Reference

Bellow, Saul, *The Bellarosa Connection* (New York: Penguin Books, 1984). Subsequent references in parentheses are to this edition.

14

Saul Bellow's Short Stories and his Last Novel

Although Bellow began his career with the small-scale works *Dangling Man* and *The Victim*, he is best known for substantial novels like *The Adventures of Augie March* and *Herzog*, and it is generally accepted that his talents are best represented in these sprawling forms. He has, however, contributed excellent short stories to periodicals as diverse as *Partisan Review* and *Playboy* and they have been reprinted in collections as *Mosby's Memories and Other Stories* (1968), *Him with His Foot in His Mouth and Other Stories* (1984) and *Something to Remember Me By: Three Tales* (1991) and again further earlier stories collections in *Collected Stories* (2001).

Mosby's Memories brings together six stories written over a period of about seventeen years, including three that were published with *Seize the Day*. Each of these three stories concerns in some way an attempt by an individual to the outside world which will allow inner and outer realities to give stable meaning to each other. The earliest, "Looking for Mr. Green" (1951), set in the bleak Chicago of the depression years, concerns the attempts of George Grebe, a displaced academic, to deliver a welfare cheque to a Mr. Green. During his journey through the black slum district he is met with suspicion and denials that make him ponder over the insubstantiality of identity and this leads him to question the possibility of establishing the existence of a stable reality. The misery and dismal ugliness of this world are one sort of reality, a product of human history and human consent, and he cannot bring himself to believe that there is not a higher reality beyond it. His quest to find Mr. Green becomes in his mind a quest for this higher reality, but when he finally finds Green's house he is confronted by a drunken, naked woman. Her refusal to either confirm or deny the presence of Mr. Green or that she is Mrs. Green appears to discredit his idea of a higher reality, but he gives her the cheque, convincing himself that Mr. Green is there, and can be found.

The protagonist of "The Gonzaga Manuscripts" (1954) also undertakes an unsuccessful but unlike Grebe he is unable to allow himself the consolation of a conviction that what he seeks is, some how, there. Clarence Feiler has gone to Spain to try to locate manuscripts of poems by a dead Spanish writer whom he admires for his positive acceptance of the world as it is and of his place as a 'creature' in it. The existence of the Gonzaga manuscripts matters to Grebe. The people he meets in his search are not interested in Gonzaga, however, and show nothing of the Gonzagian spirit that Feiler so values, being more concerned with the weaknesses of Gonzaga's flesh, and assuming that Feiler's own concerns with the poet must be materialistic. Be numbered by his experience, he has to abandon not only his quest but also the vision of human possibility that it has held out for him.

The material burden of the world weighs heavily on Rogin, the protagonist of "A Father-to-Be" (1955), in a different way. He is oppressed by his financial commitments to his brother and his mother, and, most of all, by the lavish spending of Joan, his finance, who is beautiful, educated and refined, but unable to find 'suitable' employment. On his way to supper at her home one evening he sees on the subway a middle-aged man who is remarkably like Joan in appearance, and imagines that this is what their son will look like in 40 year's time. But the man is all that Rogin despises: fourth rate, ordinary, dull, self-satisfied and fundamentally bourgeois; and Rogin becomes enraged at the injustice of this, the fact that his personal aims should count for nothing in the creation of the future, and also resentful at Joan for this further pressure he thinks she has imposed on him. When he arrives at her house, however, she persuades him to let her wash his hair, and overwhelmed by her female tenderness he abandons his determination to assert himself. Like the two other stories, "A Father-to-Be" is concerned in part with the crushing weight of the material on the human spirit. In all of them money is the source of the denial of this higher humanity: Grebe tries to hold on to a vision of something ulterior to the physical reality that money has created, Feiler's idealism is extricably bound up with an idea of artistic value that is exploded by his discovery of the acquisitive and destructive interests of those he confronts; Rogin, worried about his own financial troubles, takes ironic comfort from the idea that all are oppressed and afflicted.

The next story "Leaving the Yellow House" was first published in 1957, while Bellow was working on *Henderson the Rain King*. It is the story Hattie Waggoner, an old woman living alone in isolated house in the Utah Desert. Faced with her own declining powers and approaching death, Hattie decides to make her will. The only thing she has to bequeath in her house which is, in a sense, her identity, she loves it, and yet it imprisons her, and its isolation is a metaphor for her own. As she considers the possible recipients of her bequest she goes back in memory over her life, finding there loss and defeat, and realizes that her only intimacy is with herself, and so in a gesture of defiance against a world that hasn't given her much she leaves her house to herself. Hattie is a large, cheerfully comic woman, both drunkenly self-destructive and resilient. She combines snobbish pride in her Philadelphia family with a desire to show herself tough enough to flourish in the Western cowboy country but the result is that she is alien in the land she inhabits. Her gesture does nothing to save her, nothing to relieve the barrenness of her existence, but it is an act of persistence; like many Bellow's heroes she insists on survival against all odds. This is a good story, and it shows Bellow experimenting with a number of things. He tentatively employs the dual/third person/first person narrative that he develops fully in *Herzog*, and he begins to explore the functions of memory. Perhaps most notably, he creates his first female protagonist; and she is not seen from a misogynist male perspective, like so many of Bellow's women, she is totally believable.

"The Old System" (1967) is completely a story of memory Dr. Samuel Barun is a biochemist whose work involves the chemistry of heredity, the science of biological connectedness and continuity. As a scientist he wants to look at life with a cold eye, to fit things into rational systems, but his story is concerned with the disordered vitality of human emotion. It begins with his love for his cousin Isaac, now dead. Isaac had offended his sister Tina over a matter of money; he was not at fault, but his sister's irrational resentment caused a rift between them. Isaac tried often to repair, but it was healed only on Tina's deathbed. Dr. Braun tries to understand this 'crude circus of feelings', and to do so he excavates his memory, tracing his family's American history to its pre-history in Russia. The story he digs up ends with a reconciliation, which he sees a reassertion of the old laws and wisdom, the old Jewish system of blood ties, of obligation and acceptance, but his own scientific system remains inadequate as a means of understanding the demands of emotional life. "The Old System" appeared while Bellow was working on *Mr. Sammler's Planet*, and it shares some of the novel's concerns; the aging Dr. Braun, lying on his December bed, considering problems of memory, meaning and mortality, foreshadows the more complex Mr. Sammler. It also takes up an issue that Bellow was later to pursue more fully in *The Dean's December* and *More Die of Heartbreak*: the ability of scientific thought to give order and meaning to human existence.

"Mosby's Memories" (1968) is the most complex of the six narratives. Willis Mosby is a retired academic and diplomat who is in Mexico writing his memories. He looks back with no small vanity on his successful career as confident and advisor to distinguished men, a career founded on his intellectual arrogance and aggressiveness. In order to avoid what he calls 'the common fate of intellectuals, the sin of pride', he decides to temper the serious stuff of his autobiography by introducing into it, as comic relief, the story of Jewish radical named Lustgarten whom he had met in post war Paris Lustgarten was a born loser, a naïve, well-meaning figure who failed in everything he did, a man doomed to be victimized by life. Mosby considers this man with detached irony and no compassion, seeing him purely as a comic figure only at the end of the story do we learn what Mosby has almost suppressed—that by making Lustgarten appear comic to his own wife as a means of seducing her, he had participated in Lustgarten's victimization. This memory triggers a wave of guilt in Mosby, expressed in a feeling of suffocation, as if he is being crushed by the realization that his stance of intellectual superiority has drained him of all humanity. Bellow provides us here with a further of the sophistication of the technique of moving in and out of the third-person narrative voice. Like the historian Henry Adams, with whom he compares himself favourably but inappropriately, Mosby thinks of himself in the third person. This is an attempt to see life objectively, but also, as it turns out, to distance himself from what he does not wish to confront: his own coldness and isolation. For all his intellectual acumen Mosby has been blind to the deeper truths of his existence, and is doomed to live out his life being what he is.

The earliest of five stories collected in *Him with His Foot in His Mouth* is "Zetland: By a Character Witness" (1974). This is hardly a story at all, it is a character sketch extracted from material developed for *Humboldt's Gift*, a memoir of the doomed poet Isaac Rosenfield. It is an affectionate portrait of the son of a Russian immigrant family. It follows him from his bookish boyhood in Chicago, where he becomes a student of philosophy, to his life in New York where, after reading Moby Dick, he decides he has to give up philosophy, moves to Greenwich Village and takes up a bohemian lifestyle, immersed in experimental literature and radical politics. Fragmentary though the story is, it builds the life of Zetland out of the piled-up detail of a rich world. If Bellow had developed the story, he would probably have clarified the character of narrator, the character witness who retrieves Zetland from his own memory, perhaps as a kind of mirror to his own life.

In most of Bellow's novels the protagonist's relationship with his father, if it exists at all, is a marginal part of the story, and is always uneasy and fractured, a source of pain in his memory, as it is for Henderson and Herzog; only in *Seize the Day* it is at the centre of the story. Like *Seize the Day*, "A Silver Dish" (1978) is the story of a man whose life is blighted by his need to be loved by a father who is incapable of giving love. Woody Selbet is a successful businessman in his sixties who attempts to come to an understanding of his relationship with his recently-deceased father. The cynically selfish Morris Selbet had abandoned his family while Woody was still a child, but had always been able to cajole money out of his son. Woody's memory fixes on an incident that had taken place forty years earlier, when his father had persuaded him to ask for money from the wealthy widow who was paying Woody's education at a seminary. Woody had reluctantly agreed, though he suspected that his father wanted the money for gambling; Morris repaid the woman's generosity by stealing a silver tray from her.

Woody tries to understand his father's action in terms of a kind of noble manhood, a refusal to accept the hypocrisy and feminine religiosity of the respectable seminary world. He needs to believe that, in some way, his father loved him, and that he himself shares some of that manhood, but in fact his father was incapable of loving anyone, and, indeed, frequently chided Woody for not being selfish enough. Woody is actually quite unlike his father, having visions of a world of love and being fully aware of his obligations to others. The story links two moments of physical struggle: Woody had grappled with his father in an attempt to make him return the silver dish but was unsuccessful; 40 years later he had grappled with him on his deathbed to prevent him from removing the tubes and needles that were keeping him alive, but Morris defeated him once again and died in his arms. Woody's real struggle, however, is with himself as he attempts to forge that impossible link: for his own emotional and spiritual equilibrium he needs to redeem a man who cannot be redeemed.

Him with His Foot in His Mouth (1982) also begins with an act of memory that instigates a self-examination. Shawmut, the narrator, is an aging intellectual, a musicologist and T.V. guru who is living in exile in British Columbia, waiting to be extradited because of his involvement in shady financial affairs. A letter from an old friend reminds him of an incident that took place 35 years before. Shawmut gratuitously insulted a librarian at the college where he was teaching and this, he is told, wounded her for life. The story is Shawmut's letter of apology to the woman, but it becomes a survey of his life and of the character traits that have led him to this exile. His insult was only one of a series of similar incidents, which he attributes to a kind of uncontrollable reflex of wit. What he reveals about himself, however, is a general ineptitude at life, and especially a failure with American materialism, that has allowed him to be swindled by his loved brother and to care for his aged mother who doesn't recognize him even though she remembers all her other children. His sense of his own value and cleverness is thus weighed against a character that has brought him to spiritual barrenness and his isolation in an alien land, and the reader's response falls between sympathy for Shawmut's loneliness and an ironic awareness of his culpability.

In each of these stories the protagonist's recollection of the past leads to a re-shaping of his life and a revelation to the reader of things that the protagonist himself does not clear understand. "Cousins" (1984) presents another, more complex account of an attempt, through memory, to reconcile past and present. Ijah Brodsky, the narrator, is an expert in law, like Shawmut an ideas-man turned television celebrity. He is asked to intercede with a judge on behalf of his cousin Tanky, and agrees to do so because of past ties. This gets him involved in the affairs of a number of other cousins. Ijah wants to feel that he is loved and admired by his cousins, though it appears that most of them, materialists that they are, have a degree of contempt for him, and are merely using him. One cousin,

Scholem, is in genuine need of Ijah's help. Scholem is the other intellectual of the family; as a youth he was a philosopher with ground-breaking ideas, and made Ijah feel inferior. He is now a taxi-driver, and seeks Ijah's help with publication of his papers, and also with securing permission to be buried in East Germany.

For all his keen intelligence, Ijah has problems. He appears to have allowed his cousins to take the place of any closer family ties, and this may have been a stratagem for distancing people rather than connecting to them, for in spite of his professed love for his cousins he has been there quite rarely; his cousin Mendy, for example, he contacts for the first time in decades, though he claims to have 'friendly and even affectionate relations' with him. He seems to have problems with closer relationships; he divorced his wife years before, and she subsequently had other husbands, but Ijah still thinks vaguely that she wants him—another example of his need of the esteem of others. The one real love of his life, a concert harpist called Virgie Dunten whom he has met perhaps five times in thirty years, is unattainable and therefore safe. Perhaps his real state of being is represented in the darkness of his apartment with its strange, oriental corners, and in his interest in Arctic exploration. His eagerness to believe in cousinly ties as representing love in the world coexists with the dark and cold of essential isolation. His final meeting with Scholem, when he suddenly realizes that he has been mistaken in his memories and his assessment of this cousin, comes a kind of epiphany, a sudden re-assessment of himself.

The next story, "What Kind of Day Did You Have?" is of interest first of all because it has in Katrina Goliger Bellow's second female protagonist. Katrina is a middle-aged woman who lives in Chicago shrub; she is going through the messy fall-out of a divorce that became necessary because of her affair with Victor Wulpy, 'a world-class intellectual, big in the art world', now in his seventies. The story covers a period of 24 hours, beginning as she is having dinner with her admirer, Sam Krieggstein, who claims to be a police lieutenant. Victor, who is giving a lecture in Buffalo, calls her to meet him there and then return with him to Chicago and although this causes her much inconvenience with her psychiatrist, her children and her housekeeper, she agrees to join him. It is a stormy day, and on the return journey they are marooned in the airport in Detroit. With growing anxiety she realizes that she will not be able to get back to Chicago before her daughters return home from school, and since she has had to lie about her trip, she fears that this will give ammunition to her vengeful ex-husband. Her fears seem to be justified when she finally gets back home and finds the house empty, and she rushes out in panic, to discover that Krieggstein has taken care of the children. She ends her day on the verge of emotional collapse.

As this line indicates, Katrina is something of a victim. She is an intelligent woman, but she has little self-esteem. She was mocked in childhood by a father who called her 'Dump Dora', and her marriage to a social climber who needed her only as a house wife gave her little opportunity to develop herself. Her envious sister Dorothea claims that Katrina has nothing to offer the intellectual high-flier but her body. Katrina half believes this, and in order to achieve some measure of independence and a sense of her own value she has been trying to write a story for children about an elephant trapped in a department store, but cannot find a way of ending it, which gives her a frustrating sense of failure. To be needed by Victor, therefore, allows her some sense of worth.

'How do you assess a woman who knows how to bind such a wizard to her?' the narrative voice asks, and the problem of this story seems to be that Katrina is valued not for anything intrinsic in her, but as she is perceived by Victor. Victor is viewed by the same narrative voice with no little admiration; words like 'wizard' and 'giant' appear frequently. At parties, the only voice to be heard is Victor's, as he monopolizes all conversations; his opinions are sought at the highest levels of political and economic activity. To the reader, however, he may appear overbearingly arrogant. He gives a talk at a university, but perceives no signs of intelligence in his audience; pursued by an old acquaintance, a successful film-maker who craves a good conversation about ideas, he is rude and hostile Katrina herself remembers with pain how she was once the recipient of his long-lasting contempt when she persuaded him to go with her to see the film Mash.

Katrina craves distinction, and she believes she is getting it by having Victor confide his thoughts in her: 'Abed, Victor and Katrina smoked, drank...they thought—my God, they thought'. But it is Victor's thinking that counts, because he doesn't listen to the thoughts of other. Indeed he has little interest in Katrina's mind, let alone respect for it: 'She could irritate him to the point of heartbreak'. He has erotic fantasies about her, she keeps him going, and this inexplicable sexual chemistry is the source of his tie to her. For all his genius, he is incapable of understanding a life different from his own, and her desire to have him say he loves her is meaningless to him; he can only respond to it with contempt. His need, perhaps, is summed in the Picasso engravings described in the story, voyeuristic depictions of old men, satyre-artists gazing at submissive female bodies ('wide-open odalisques').

Katrina wants to grow, to break out of the self defined by her father and her husband, and Victor's demanding intellectual company seems to be a way for her to do that. But the assumption of her inferiority by both Victor and herself means that she remains in the trap. She is like the elephant in her story, and is no more capable of extricating herself than she is of freeing the elephant. "What Kind of Day Did You Have?" has much sympathy for Katrina, yet we cannot help feeling, as we read, that Bellow's real interest is with Victor Wulpy.

"What Kind of Day Did You Have?" is much more substantial than the other stories in this collection; it is really a novella. It is as long as *Seize the Day*, as long as the later work *A Theft*, with which it has much in common. Bellow, late in his career, seems to have turned away from the sprawling novels that are generally taken to be his forte to the cleaner lines for these shorter forms. The central issues of his larger novels are still here, but the extended presentation of ideas in the novels from *Herzog* onwards is not possible, and there is less room for the didacticism, the lecturing that for many readers mars his major work.

In his illuminating lecture on "The Short Story Element in Bellow's Fiction" Earl Rovit pointed to the story as the "core element" of all Bellow's creative work. Bellow creates his novels from an abundance of stories, interlocking stories within stories or connecting them in sequences according to the principle of the "comic strip plot structure". As it were Rovit who perceived Bellow's cumulative art as based on an inductive method which may be correlated in part to Bellow's intense preoccupation with the social sciences. This method would explain, Rovit holds, Bellow's "increasing reliance on plotlessness". As a striking paradigm of Bellow's creative method of combining stories, Rovit aptly referred to the genesis of the novel *Humboldt's Gift*, in which two stories were interlaced.

The story, however, must not be seen genetically only as the "core element" of Bellow's expansive novelist writing. Bellow himself has always taken the story very seriously as an independent work of art in its own right. Bellow stressed emphatically his long-standing genuine interest and endeavours in short narratives, which he feels are particularly suitable for the modern lifestyle. In these endeavours Bellow had been repeatedly encouraged by his close friend and fictional advisor, Richard G. Stern.

Ravelstein (2000), Bellow's last novel written at the age of eighty-five, tells the tale of a friendship between two university professors and the complications that animate their erotic attachments well into old age. The title character is based on Allan Bloom who taught with Bellow at the University of Chicago's Committee on Social Thought. The story follows the physical decline of Ravelstein and how his recent literary fame and financial success impacted his life. After Ravelstein's death, the remainder of the work deals with the narrator's own illness and hospitalization. Ravelstein is not aloof or uninterested by the Martin Heidegger—like 'fallen-ness' of everyday life. He is a consumer of goods and gossip, eagerly meeting people where they exist, without constructing artificial barriers based on presumed superiority. His friendships do not solely revolve around his own interests and concerns. Thoughts and opinions expressed by Ravelstein are often humorous, precisely because they are so 'common' and 'cliched'. Upon lighting a cigarette to open a class, he mentions that students who dislike tobacco more than they love ideas, will not be missed. He even rearranges the love lives of his students, often without being asked, going so far as to ask them to return with any gossip that isn't treason to repeat.

Bellow depicts Ravelstein as one of the few remaining Renaissance men in modern universities. The professor, turned best-selling author, works to counter the impoverishment of the contemporary 'market place of ideas', even if he is a little too attached to his own passions and personal vanity. Chick contrasts with Ravelstein as an older fellow more cautious and predictable. When he claims he is saving Proust for the nursing home, Ravelstein asks why wait? Intellectual honesty binds these friends.

Bellow asks in *Ravelstein* how one is best remembered: for contributions to the general knowledge; for contributions to humanity via one's fellow-treatment of one's friends, intimates, and stranger, or for the rate at which one's notoriety attracts mass attention and thereafter decays. That last theme is poignantly exhibited in two instances. Early in a chance encounter between Ravelstein and Chick with pop star Michael Jackson and his entourage at Paris Hotel Crillon and later when Ravelstein recalls following Elizabeth Taylor through an airport terminal as a sudden and quickly departing obsession. Bellow, in *Ravelstein*, reveals the cross cuttings of purpose and truth in the trajectories of remembrance. In this pattern of coming and going Bellow seems to imply, the best recalling of a man, is a complete depiction of complication and chance painted against the higher ambition of shared existence. What is left out of this story is any reckoning with eternity in the face of impending death, or the religious element of human life. This is consistent with Bellow's modernization of the Jewish experience in North American twentieth century culture.

The novel was controversial in its frank depiction of Ravelstein as a gossipmonger, frivolous spender, influence peddler, petty complainer, promiscuous panderer, and homosexual dying from AIDS related complications in a relationship with a much younger man. Despite all these faults, Ravelstein remains a valued friend and colleague whose illness and passing is considered a tragic loss to his friends and admirers, but never diminished his own love of life. But Bellow revealed that Bloom, a philosopher and social critic aligned with many American conservative ideas and ambitions, was anything but conservative in his private life. Accordingly, some took the book; however, Bellow vigorously rejected speculations, citing many conversations between Bloom and himself where the subject urged 'a warts and all' tell all about him. Bloom was not a 'closeted' homosexual, for many of his friends, colleagues and former students knew of his sexual orientation; although he never publicly spoke of it. He was a bachelor and never married or had children. He criticized 'the homosexual', in his book *Closing of American Mind*, in American Universities.

Index

E

F

G

H

J

K

L

M